HOW YOUR PERSONALITY TYPE IS INHERITED: THE NPA MODEL OF GENETIC TRAITS

HOW YOUR PERSONALITY TYPE IS INHERITED:

THE NPA MODEL OF GENETIC TRAITS

A.M. BENIS, Sc.D., M.D.

A.M. BENIS
New York

KDP edition

ISBN 978-1-521-37103-9

Internet site: npatheory.com

When you cannot measure it, when you cannot express it in numbers, you have scarcely, in your thoughts, advanced to the stage of Science, whatever the matter may be.

— Lord Kelvin (1883)

CONTENTS

ILLUSTRATIONS & TABLES

PREFACE

As the title suggests, the purpose of this book is to allow you, the reader, to see how your personality type was inherited. That's right, we are talking specifically about *your* personality, the personality that you were born with and which you will keep for the rest of your life.

Our approach is direct, precise and quantitative. If you were expecting vague argumentation about feel-good issues, or a confirmation of the idea that we are all blank slates when we are born, subject only to the molding influences of environment, then this is perhaps not the book for you.

By inheritance, we mean the genes that you received from your parents. Our premise is that humans have several major personality traits resulting from just a few genes, and that we can trace the traits in a family pedigree. By personality type, we mean that the traits assort themselves — one, two or three traits together — so that every individual has cohesive set of physical and behavioral qualities that can be recognized as a discrete "type". There are three basic traits and about a dozen common personality types. Although we use some symbols and do some arithmetical computations, it's not all that complicated.

For those already familiar with the NPA model, the most interesting portion of this book is likely to be Chapter 8, where we consider twenty "case studies" that illustrate how the personality traits are transmitted. Here, you will meet Giovanni and Pania, Bogdan and Lulu, as well as King Lucifer IV and his many mistresses. Each of the illustrations has an instructive element, and when you are through with this chapter, you should be in good form to do your own analysis… of yourself, your family, your significant other, and even of children who are not yet born.

The three NPA traits of sanguinity, perfectionism and aggression were first advanced as a group by Karen Horney in the 1950's ("We must consider at least three subdivisions of the 'expansive type': the narcissistic, the perfectionistic and the arrogant-vindictive type.") Horney's interpretation of her three types was that they were the result of stressful *environment*, but this is understandable, since her training was in psychoanalysis, and the age of genetics had not yet arrived. If Horney had lived to our more modern era, it is likely that she would have wholeheartedly embraced a genetic explanation for the three traits. Very likely, she would have found great satisfaction in the idea that they are not behavioral maladaptations due to onerous environment, but rather basic structural elements of the human personality.

The NPA model has a number of speculative elements that need confirmation, so we cannot guarantee that all of its predictions will be verified. However, we can guarantee that you will not be bored. In fact, for some people the NPA model has been an exciting journey, and perhaps the same will be true for you as well.

AMB
20 August 2018.

1

Personality Is Inherited

THE purpose of this book is to present a concise summary by which you, the reader, can analyze your genetically determined personality type in the context of your own family. This book should be especially accessible to those who already know the "NPA" scheme by which we categorize personality type. However, for those not familiar with the model, the first five chapters are intended to be a brief introduction to bring you up to speed quickly.

If you are analytically oriented, you will find that you will readily be able to identify specific traits in yourself and in members of your family: in parents, siblings, and in uncles and aunts. You will be able to sketch out a "family pedigree", or tree, in which each member of your family is labeled with a distinct personality type, and you will be able to see how a particular trait is transmitted from one generation to the next. If you are a parent, or plan to become one, and you ascertain the personality type of your mate, then you can use this information to narrow down the possible personality types in your children — including those as yet unborn.

Yes, personality is inherited

Human personality is a complex entity, and there has been a multitude of efforts to define and measure it. Most definitions of personality are something like "a collection of emotional, thought and behavioral patterns unique to a person that is consistent over time" [1].

It is common knowledge that personality traits are, to a degree, heritable. Everybody knows that identical twins are not only "identical" with regard to physical features, but similar in personality as well. And everyone knows instances where a child is a "spitting image" of one of the parents. And by this it is meant that the son or daughter not only looks like, but remarkably behaves like one of the parents.

Scientifically speaking, personality research has not made much progress in the past decades. There are a great many theories of personality, which means that there is no consensus as to which approach is the correct one. Most of the concepts are fuzzy and empirical —"three from column A and four from column B" — and not amenable to being either proved or disproved.

As things stand at present, the conventional wisdom of the research community is that *many, many genes* contribute to personality, and the complexity is such that *no gene* contributes more than a few percent of the effect in any aspect of human behavior. As a result, there is currently little effort being made to identify specific genetic personality traits and to incorporate them into a model of personality. The conventional wisdom has firmly established the politically correct illusion that the human personality is so complex that every child is effectively a "blank slate" at birth, capable of being molded into any conceivable configuration by parental nurture, education and other aspects of environment.

Unfortunately, the above conventional wisdom is utterly wrong, and it will eventually be shown to be false by geneticists, probably in the not too distant future. In fact, we can easily show that it is false from common experience. We all know of instances where a child has a "personality type" just like one of the parents — who themselves may be very different. It is a very common occurrence. There are striking examples of this in my family and very likely in yours as well. Now, if *many genes* were involved, a child's inheriting the "entire packet" of personality genes from just one of the parents would be an extremely rare event! After all, the "many" genes would be scattered on that parent's more than twenty pairs of chromosomes, and since a child inherits only one chromosome of each pair, how could "all of the many genes" be transmitted together?

The "NPA model" that we use to trace traits in a family pedigree is the only "trait model" of personality proposed to date that is based on classical genetics. In our experience, the model corresponds closely to reality and explains why so often a child's personality is so similar to that of one of the parents. However, the NPA traits have not yet been researched by geneticists, so any results that the model produces must be cautiously termed as theoretical or provisional. But the potential of the NPA model is unique: it is the only theory of personality that proposes to make an assessment of the personality types of children according to the personality types of the parents. Specifically, if one can identify the specific NPA types of the parents, then one can predict the potential types of the children, sometimes narrowing down the possibilities to just one or two types.

The three-trait model

The NPA model was developed on the basis of concepts clarified over sixty years ago by psychiatrist Karen Horney. According to the model, there are three major, genetically determined, character traits that form the basis of personality. The traits are *sanguinity* (N), *perfectionism* (P) and *aggression* (A). The traits are multifaceted, or in formal terms, each one dependent on a "pleiotropic gene" by which a single gene can cause a complex pattern of aspects related to behavior.

The letter N is used to denote sanguinity because it is related to the classic concept of "narcissism".

In simple terms, A is the "power trait", N is the "glory trait", and P is a "modulator trait" that modifies or tempers the expression of the A and N traits.

The two traits, A and N, represent human ambition to attain power and glory. Every individual must have a measure of trait A, or trait N, or both.

An individual's NPA personality type is solely determined by the combination of N, P and A traits that he or she has inherited from the parents. It is not all that complicated, as there are only three traits with which we have to deal. There are about a dozen common NPA personality types.

Egg and sperm donation

It is understood that it is the *biological parents* who solely determine the NPA type of a child. If one of the biological parents is an egg or sperm donor, then the NPA type of that donor is just as important in the determination of the child's personality type as is the type of the other parent.

It's all about you

In the next four chapters we introduce the three traits of the model and show how different combinations of the traits lead to very real "personality types" that anyone can learn to recognize. Next, we focus on how the traits are transmitted genetically from parents to a child, thus determining the innate personality type that the child will carry for his or her entire life.

And, since you, too, were once a child, we can say that this book is, in a very literal sense... all about you.

2

Three Traits: N, P and A

The NPA model of personality was developed on the basis of concepts advanced by German-American psychiatrist Karen Horney during the mid-twentieth century [2]. According to the theory, there are three major genetically determined character traits that form the basis of personality. The traits are *sanguinity* (N), *perfectionism* (P) and *aggression* (A).

An important premise of the model is that in any individual either the trait N or A, or both, must be expressed.

The three traits

Sanguinity (N) is the trait of sociability. Individuals with the trait tend to be prone to flushing, blushing and tearfulness. A hallmark of the trait is the *gingival smile* broadly exposing gums and teeth [3]. In the extreme, the trait appears as a "search for glory", and individuals may display vanity, exhibitionism and show overt narcissistic behavior. Individuals having trait N are called "sanguine" types and sometimes, appropriately, "narcissistic" types.

Aggression (A) is the well-known trait of competitiveness, often physical in nature. Individuals having the A trait (but lacking the N trait) tend to be inhibited in sociability and in flushing, blushing, tearfulness and smiling. In the extreme, the trait is a "search for power", and individuals may display physical confrontation, pugnacity and show overtly sadistic behavior. Individuals with the trait of aggression instinctively form "pecking orders". Individuals having trait A but lacking trait N are called "non-sanguine" types.

Perfectionism (P) is a trait that may or may not be present in a given individual. It may be thought of as modulating the N and A traits. Individuals having overt expression of the P trait tend to value order, neatness and symmetry, and may be prone to repetitive mannerisms. In the extreme, the trait may be the cause of obsessive-compulsive or autistic-like behavior that may overwhelm other character traits. Individuals lacking trait P are called "non-perfectionistic".

Traits A and N are associated with rage reactions, namely the classic "aggressive-vindictive rage" (A rage) associated with pallor in individuals of light skin color, and the florid "narcissistic rage" (N rage) associated with sanguinity. The P trait is not associated with a rage reaction.

The traits A and N form the basis of human ambition, namely the desire to achieve power and glory, respectively.

An important result is that the model produces a limited number of discrete character types, according to how the three traits are assorted, and whether the traits are present, absent, or incompletely expressed. On the assumption that the three traits are transmitted independently from parents to child, we identify three main categories of personality types: 1) Dominant, 2) Inhibited Aggressive, and 3) Borderline.

The NPA personality types

1. Dominant types

In the case that all three traits are either absent or fully expressed, we obtain the following types:

N   sanguine
A   non-sanguine aggressive
NA   sanguine aggressive
NP   sanguine perfectionistic
PA   non-sanguine perfectionistic aggressive
NPA   sanguine perfectionistic aggressive

The types are denoted *sanguine* or *non-sanguine* depending on the presence or absence of the trait N, respectively. The two Dominant non-sanguine types are A and PA.

The types are denoted *aggressive* or *non-aggressive* depending on the presence or absence of the trait A. The two Dominant non-aggressive types are N and NP.

Thus, there are four sanguine and two non-sanguine Dominant types, as well as four aggressive and two non-aggressive Dominant types.

2. Inhibited Aggressive types

There are two divisions of Inhibited Aggressive types, designated a) *Passive Aggressive* and b) *Resigned* types.

a. Passive Aggressive types

If trait A is partially inhibited *genetically from birth*, we obtain the category of Passive Aggressive types. The term "passive aggressive" here simply means that expression of trait A is partially inhibited, and it does not imply "passive-aggressive behavior" in any pejorative sense. We append one minus sign (–) or two minus signs (=) to the letter A, according to whether trait A is only partially or profoundly inhibited.

We obtain the following Passive Aggressive types:

NPA– NPA= sanguine perfectionistic
NA– NA= sanguine non- perfectionistic

Passive Aggressive types may be prone to submissive behavior. For identification, we call the A= types *compliant* types and the A– types *non-compliant* types. In dominant-submissive relationships, non-compliant types can play either the dominant or submissive role, depending on the partner, while compliant types will always seek to play the subservient role.

b. Resigned types

If trait A is inhibited because of *environmental constraints after maturity*, we obtain the category of avoidance, or resignation. Unlike Passive Aggressive types who readily involve themselves in the relative competition of dominance and submission (and sometimes sadomasochism), Resigned types remain detached from such activities and only with difficulty can be stressed to a competitive, energetic state of aggression.

Denoting the state of resignation by –A, we obtain the following Resigned types:

NP–A   sanguine perfectionistic
N–A   sanguine non-perfectionistic

3. Borderline types

Borderline types are those in whom neither trait N nor trait A is fully expressed [4]. These constrained types are relatively uncommon and are not explored in detail in this book. For further information on this category and its possible relation to mental illness, see Appendix A.

The N and A rages

The occurrence of the N and A rages is possible in any of the types having the N and A traits, respectively. The rages are typically triggered by stressful environmental circumstances during an individual's daily life. The two rages can occur together, synergistically, in the "NA rage" if both the N and A traits are present in the individual's NPA type.

In the Passive Aggressive and Resigned types, the trait A of aggression is inhibited but nonetheless present, so like the Dominant types, these types can exhibit the A rage. Typically, however, in the context of generally repressed aggression and a life style of deference or avoidance in social relations, the actual occurrence of the A rage in these types is likely to be unusual.

In contrast, the non-aggressive N and NP types are genetically completely inhibited from exhibiting the A rage of aggression, just as the non-sanguine A and PA types lack the capacity to exhibit the N rage of sanguinity.

Complexities: other genes and environment

Biological variability and outliers

Just as all males and all females are not alike, there is considerable variability in the behavioral characteristics of a given genetic NPA type. This is basically because of 1) "genes other than the NPA genes" that influence behavior, and 2) environment.

In the extreme, one should be aware that "outliers" can certainly exist. An outlier is an individual of a certain NPA type who has some unusual attributes that seem "out of character" for that particular type. There are two main reasons for outliers. First, the individual may have an unusual "other gene" that rarely occurs in the general population, or the individual may have been exposed to an unusual set of environmental conditions. Second, the individual may simply have an unusual combination, or "perfect storm", of commonly occurring genes or environmental exposures.

Thus, the NPA traits are only a basic structural skeleton of the human personality, with many other factors, both genetic and environmental, possibly contributing to biological variability in the various NPA types. Among these are *basic drives* (hunger, thirst, sex, territoriality), *cognition* (thinking, learning, reasoning, intelligence), *temperament* (the natural activity or excitability of an individual), as well as other less clearly defined human traits, like empathy and altruism. *Environmental variables* like nurture, culture, and the individual's real-life situation in society provide a final overlay of complexity.

Relationships of dominance and submission

In social interactions a Dominant character type having the A trait has the potential of adopting a *subdued or subjugated state* $A-$ if the particular individual is dominated by a stronger partner. In this state, the Dominant individual would exhibit behaviorisms similar to a Passive Aggressive type. Similarly, a Passive Aggressive type has the potential of being activated to an *energetic state* $A+$ resembling dominance. Thus, the model emphasizes the potential lability of the A trait, with Dominant and

Passive Aggressive types continually altering their behavior in competitive interactions with other individuals and in the context of mating.

The model emphasizes that from the point of view of inheritance, we need to focus on an individual's baseline genetic NPA type, not on the individual's environmentally influenced social behavior that may vary from day to day.

Temperament as a facet of personality

One of the most important aspects of the genetics of personality in the category of "genes other than the NPA genes" is the notion of temperament. By this, we mean the *general activity or reactivity* of an individual, as in the sense that it is applied in regard to domesticated animals, such as dogs or horses. Thus, a particular individual, say a Dominant NP type, could be described to have a "high temperament" or a "low temperament".

The concept of temperament has not been adequately investigated, or even appreciated, in the behavioral sciences. In the NPA model we make the simplest assumption: that the genes that underlie temperament are separate from the NPA genes, hence that the NPA personality type of an individual can be determined irrespective of his or her innate level of temperament.

The "television set" analogy

One can think of an individual's personality in terms of the analogy of viewing a television receiver. If there were only two basic models of television sets, then this would represent the *male-female dichotomy*: The *NPA personality type* would then be the channel selector, *temperament* would be the volume control, and how well the TV picture is actually visualized would depend on the lighting in the room, or *environment*.

While acknowledging the complexity of personality in the broader sense of the term, including the above concept of temperament, our model implies that it is the *male-female dichotomy* and the *NPA personality type* that comprise the highest genetic tiers of the human personality structure. Specifically, despite the complexities of "biological variability", we can nevertheless identify an individual's unique genetic NPA type.

Profiles of the NPA types

In next three chapters, we present profiles of the most common NPA character types. The profiles are excerpts from our prior work [5], where the descriptions were presented mainly in the form of *caricatures*. The reason for the use of caricatures was that it allowed us to focus on the specific characteristics, and foibles, of the various NPA types without any implication that the descriptions are to be taken literally or pejoratively.

In fact, our view is that none of the NPA types are presented to be any better or worse than any other. Sometimes a particular behavioral characteristic that seems unfavorable in one social context turns out to be quite advantageous in another. Humans are cognitive beings, and as we stressed above, there is much more to personality and individual behavior than just being male or female, or having a particular assortment of the NPA traits.

Following Karen Horney, we sometimes use gender-specific pronouns to describe the various types, although the descriptions apply both to males and females. Unfortunately, in the English language there is no good way to avoid this.

Generalizations

Despite our appreciation of the complications of "biological variability", we attempted in the profiles to identify trends for such categories as *complexion, gestures, handwriting, sexuality*, and so on. These generalizations should be viewed with caution, since they are, at best, trends in a statistical sense, and could not be used to infer anything about a particular individual. These "trends" have not been confirmed in any scientific sense.

In addition, in the context of population genetics, we comment on where we believe the various NPA types to be most prevalent worldwide. We introduce the term *habitancy* to describe localized subpopulations of particular distributions of NPA types in various geographical regions [6].

Finally, we include a category called *pitfalls*. This is a comment on how a particular NPA type might be confused with a different type. There are many reasons why confusion between two types might arise, but a primary reason is that two different types can overlap in one, or even two, of the NPA traits.

[DonkeyHotey & Carsten S.]

Fig. 1. Caricatures of the six Dominant types. *L to R, from top:* N, A, NP, PA, NPA and NA.

3

Dominant Types

The first major category of NPA types is that of the *Dominant types,* where the three traits are either absent or all fully expressed. Thus, there are six types:

N   sanguine
A   non-sanguine aggressive
NA   sanguine aggressive
NP   sanguine perfectionistic
PA   non-sanguine perfectionistic aggressive
NPA   sanguine perfectionistic aggressive

The N, NA, NP and NPA types are the *sanguine* types, meaning that they have the N trait. The A and PA types are called *non-sanguine* types.

The A, NA, PA and NPA are the *aggressive* types, meaning that they have the A trait. The N and NP types are called *non-aggressive* types.

The NP, PA and NPA types are the *perfectionistic* types, meaning that they have the P trait. The N, A and NA types are called *non-perfectionistic* types. These latter three types, where neither trait N nor A is tempered by the P trait, are prone to what we term "unbridled narcissism" or "unbridled aggression".

The pure N and A types

The N type and the A type may be regarded to be "pure" types, in the sense that they are the only types having just a single NPA trait that is not influenced by the other two traits. Thus, the traits of sanguinity and aggression can be best appreciated in the N and A types. It is in these typically extroverted individuals that we can appreciate the unfettered extremes of human behavior that have their roots in the N and A traits. For the N trait, these extremes lie in vanity, exhibitionism and narcissism, or "narcissistic personality disorder". For the A trait, the extremes lie in coerciveness, brutishness and sadism, or "antisocial personality disorder".

The N and A traits together

The N and A traits are present together, fully expressed, in the NA type. The two traits tend not to interfere with each other or modify each other. Rather, they appear together in an unchanged or synergistic manner, so that the NA type is typically an active, highly extroverted, non-perfectionistic individual where full-blown unbridled narcissism and aggression are both on display.

The bridling effect of the P trait: NP and PA types

The effect of the presence of the P trait on the N and A traits can be profound. The effect on the N trait is such that instead of an outgoing N individual prone to vanity, the result is a less extroverted NP individual prone to perfectionistic, obsessive compulsiveness. The effect on the A trait is such that instead of an outgoing A individual prone to overt brutishness, the result is a less extroverted PA individual prone to repressed aggressive behavior.

When all three N, P and A traits are present

The individual having all three traits together, fully expressed, is the NPA Dominant type (sometimes denoted as the *NPA+* type for clarity).

The resultant effect of all three traits being present together may be appreciated by imagining "adding the P trait" to the behavior of the NA type. The effect is a tempering one, but the result is still an extroverted individual who may be prone to excesses characteristic of the both the N and A traits acting in concert. The outward effects of the N and A traits may be so overt that although these individuals may consider themselves to be "perfectionists", this may not be the opinion of others. That is, the N and A traits acting together may mask the presence of the P trait as a modulating trait in the sense of "perfectionism".

Profiles

Below are brief summaries of the six Dominant types:

N type

"Sanguine type"

Sanguine, non-perfectionistic, non-aggressive type

N types are typically extroverted, sanguine complexioned, non-perfectionistic, and prone to narcissistic posturing and adornment. Low temperament individuals can be soft-spoken, gallant or angelic. High temperament individuals can be charismatic, or intrusive, overbearing and brash. The N type is quite common in politics, aristocratic families and in all lists of famous people, especially in the arts.

Rage: Narcissistic "N rage" (florid rage resembling a childish tantrum).

Also known as: "Narcissistic type". Charismatic personality. The self-anointed glory seeker. "Narcissus".

Complexion: Sanguine, florid, flushed to blood-red in individuals of light skin color. Blushes easily.

Smile: Radiant "gingival" smile, broadly exposing gums and teeth.

Photograph: Looks at camera. Broad charismatic gingival smile. Starry-eyed smile.

Voice: Confident, smooth, unctuous, pontificating.

Gestures: Deep bow, accompanied by sweeping arm. "Narcissistic arms gesture" in which the arms are extended to the front or sides, with the palms up and the fingers somewhat spread apart. It is a pose often assumed by singers and by religious leaders. "Joan of Arc pose" in which the individual's eyes are directed toward the heavens when accepting recognition in the limelight.

Handwriting: Very variable. May be beautifully well formed with flourishes, but non-perfectionistic. May be illegible scribbling, especially in male. Exhibitionistic signature ("John Hancock") is common.

Sexuality: Tendency to promiscuity: high. Tendency to LGBT in sexual orientation: relatively high.

Color preference: Red, especially deep red, is the favorite color of the N type.

Population genetics: "The Sublime Habitancy", having a high prevalence of N types, some NP types, and very few types having the trait of aggression. Examples: South Sea Islanders, natives of Hawaii, indigenous East Africa and southern Asia.

Susceptibilities: Narcissistic personality disorder (NPD), megalomania. Unfocused personality. Attention deficit disorders (ADD, ADHD). Borderline personality disorder. Confidence man/woman. Vagabond. Munchausen syndrome. Congenital or rheumatic heart disease. CVA (stroke). Eating disorders. Bipolar depression. Down's syndrome parent.

Pitfalls: Until the lack of compulsive perfectionism becomes apparent, N types can resemble NP types. High temperament N types can mimic NA types or NPA+ types. N types with insipient psychosis can exhibit behavior that resembles aggression. Violence in sociopathic N types can lead to mistaken conclusion of A trait.

Character caricature [7]

He would convey the impression that "I will be the greatest, the most glorious and the most beautiful, and in fact I think that I already am!" He is self-admiring. He has great ambitions with regard to future accomplishments, but does not recognize his limitations. His eyes are set more toward himself and toward the limelight of recognition to be attained in the future than toward the actual tasks with which he must deal. His voice is soothing and clear, and may be directed toward the horizon where all can hear it. His pride is also invested in the beauty of his physical body when in the presence of others. With his not so subtle body postures, mannerisms, and self-congratulatory laughter, he flaunts himself.

Lacking perfectionist qualities, he may have difficulties in organizing himself. He lacks persistence or staying power. Perfectionism by careful repetitive action is alien to him. He has no aggressive-vindictive qualities, does not "play the game" of dominance and submission and does not become involved in the dependency of subjugation. He does not split his personality to a subdued state. He cannot be incited into an aggressive-vindictive rage.

He cannot tolerate any serious criticism of his qualities, or interference in his ambition to attain the limelight. When frustrated he may, on the one hand, be incited into the narcissistic "N rage" of defense and withdrawal, or on the other hand, he may undergo a depression to an abject state of hopelessness...

Note that we have discovered the personality type of the *proselytizing evangelist* or the *self-anointed prophet*. The important qualities of such a personality are as follows. First, he does not recognize his limitations, and his glorious goals become frank delusions of grandeur. Second, lacking perfectionist qualities, he does not occupy himself with the fine details of the means by which his goals are to be attained. For this he requires disciples and other followers to rally around him for the Cause. Third, he is self-anointed; thus, in glorifying his Cause, he is in inverted terms glorifying himself. Finally, lacking aggressive qualities, he is not only sexually unaggressive but also essentially defenseless against attack. If brought before a tribunal he can only repeat in direct or inverted terms that he is the anointed one. And if maltreated and physically abused, he can but turn the other cheek. If led to the gibbet or burned at stake, the anointed one will die the death of a passive martyr, all the while hearing inner voices reassuring him that in the glory of his death lies the glory of his purpose in life...

He is the epitome of unbridled narcissism. Hence, his complexion tends to be sanguine and his smile sublime. If he is at all handsome or beautiful, or even if he is not, he will adorn himself in finery. The female, especially, will not be able to resist wearing colorful clothes or painting her face in a manner that may startle onlookers. If the opportunity arises to flaunt his body in the nude, or semi-nude, he will not be able to resist it. Thus, he displays immense vanity with regard to personal appearance, for example in matters of cleanliness and hair style, but there his punctiliousness stops. In other matters, we shall see, he is flamboyant and extravagant, but as he rides his tiger through life he never seems to achieve any true sense of order or stability.

In placid circumstances this individual is a friendly, unaggressive, perennially optimistic, often charming individual who becomes radiant like a sunflower when flattered. Rather than be embarrassed by adulation, he will revel in it. Whatever his station in life, he will not be able to resist the temptation to mount the podium if the opportunity presents itself. If he has even mediocre talent, he will be a compulsive jokester, a mimic, an amateur singer, or will play some kind of musical instrument. If he has real talent or physical beauty, he will be inexorably drawn to a career in the field of fashion modeling, in the performing arts or in show business. Alternatively he may be drawn to any one of the professions where public oratory is possible. He may thus be a politician, a social activist or an evangelist. As an engineer, a businessman or a physician his genuinely friendly manner may mystify those with whom he comes in contact. They may think his extroverted affectations to be somewhat strange, and may consider him to be either incredibly naive, incredibly conceited or simply groutheaded.

If he inverts his mannerisms of self-importance, he shows no trace of conceit. He presents himself as a dedicated individual with a soothing, self-assured manner. The male may have a starry-eyed appearance and may be accused of being elfish, effeminate or "flaky". The female may be described as "angelic" or "dreamy". If his voice is loud, which it often is in the male, it is a voice of hollowness rather than forcefulness, as if it were a clarion call being delivered into the void around him

Although he is not predatory in a sexual manner, he is extremely vulnerable to flattery and may seek adulation. Hence, he is prone to attracting sycophantic parasites and may even develop intimate physical relations with adulators of the same sex. He may present himself as a sexually promiscuous person but in a naive and ingenuous manner. More than sexual pleasure, he needs the constant reassurance of the opposite sex that he is indeed the wonderful person of his dreams. To others, therefore, he appears to have the amorality of innocence, rather than of vice.

As an unaggressive individual, the N type may, at first blush, be confused with the NP type. However, the NP type tends to be poker-faced or melancholic, and tends to work alone in a perfectionistic manner. The N individual, on the contrary, tends to be buoyant, self-assured, jocular, expansive or even charismatic, and tends to seek people out in order to enlist their aid in his projects. Thus, the NP individual will work quietly to solve a particular problem, while the N individual will organize a conference so that he may lead a discussion on how his ideas may be implemented.

In competitive society, it may be difficult to avoid him, for although he is not aggressive he is obtrusive. He may precede his visit with a letter, definitely written in the first person, describing his extraordinary talents, the fine things that he has done in the past, despite all odds against him, and the grand things that he hopes to accomplish, nay will accomplish. He stands proud, tends to flaunt his body, and projects his resonant voice not only to his partner in conversation, but also to anyone within earshot, or even beyond. His objectives may be grandiose and far beyond the limits of reasonableness in relation to his present status in life.

Any new activity or new person arriving on the scene arouses his great interest, and he will not be able to resist imposing himself on others, ostensibly to see if he can help. And he wishes to help because he believes that he has the qualities and talents to help. On close examination, though, it is he who desires assistance, and his favors done to others reflect this ulterior motive, especially with regard to long-range assistance in his career. And in the background, deep in his unconscious mind, there lives a pervasive suspicion that perhaps all those glorious deeds will never come to fruition. Hence, he requires constant reassurance from others of his worth to them.

What emerges in this character type is an individual who has everything invested in the attainment of the fruits of his ambition, namely in the attainment of the limelight. However, lacking perfectionist qualities, he lacks the ability to apply himself to the finer details of the tasks to be done. This may not be obvious to others at first because he does indeed have boundless energy, and he may seem to have endless "persistence" when it comes to adorning himself or his abode to "perfection", often to the point of garishness. And, it is true, he may be an enthusiastic author when it comes to writing his autobiography or other epic, soaring literary efforts that glorify himself in direct or in barely camouflaged inverted terms. Nevertheless, despite such occasional activities of self-glorification, where he appears to be motivated, dynamic and goal oriented, on closer examination he lacks the persistence to create a meaningful synthesis of the mass of interrelated details that surround him. He is vague. He may be grossly, illogically imprudent. He has infinite pride in being recognized for his nebulous "creativity". But he is like a Don Quixote who leaps onto his horse and tries to gallop off in four directions at once.

For the N type the ends justify the means, and in fact, he would rather not have to bother with the means at all! We see, then, that he judges people not even so much for their potential for future accomplishments as for their already proven abilities to deliver the goods to him. And, of course, his estimation of others varies in direct proportion to the reassurance, deference and outright flattery that they give him.

Having so much invested in attainment of the limelight, once he arrives there it may be difficult to ease him out. His showmanship may take precedence over virtually all other aspects of his character. He may, then, neglect the accepted modalities of human decorum, as he talks endlessly in the first person, and in so doing he inevitably begins to neglect the truth.

Finally, he is vulnerable in the limelight and may be self-destructive there. If he is a sports figure, he may risk his life in attempting a dazzling but dangerous play. And it is he, of course, who will perform the most courageous of courageous acts if they are done in the presence of others, but will be strangely immobile if his noble deed would remain unknown to them.

At work he flaunts himself with his unctuous manner, his ostentatious handwriting and his mellifluous voice. In meetings he arouses resentment in others when he speaks of himself in overt or inverted terms. If others protest, he will not know what they are talking about, for he is the anointed one. And if he is seriously criticized or otherwise frustrated, he will explode into the red-faced narcissistic rage of defense: "I, in fact, am the only one who does anything worthwhile around here!" and of withdrawal: "If you people don't appreciate me, I'm leaving!"

He does not "play the game" of dominance and submission and is not overtly vindictive. If he does raise his voice in frustration to reprimand someone, his bark is but a hollow bellow, and everyone knows it. He is usually a person who would not hurt a fly. His love relations are not based on subjugation but on his conviction of his own beauty, his sexual wiles, and his irresistibility. And in his self-glorification he shows his Achilles heel, for he may become less able to interact meaningfully with those around him, and more and more a prisoner of his own inflated image of himself.

Nevertheless, an individual of the N type may, despite the constraints of his character structure, achieve great success in life. Although lacking the behavioral trait of perfectionism, his narcissistic drive for achievement may allow him to arrive at real accomplishments, especially if his perennial optimism can attract others to help him bring to fruition those dazzling visions of future triumphs.

Those of his acquaintances who do not know him well will be among those who like him the least. They will titter behind his back for his unctuous manner, his conceit, his extravagance and his frivolousness. They may ridicule him for his affected charisma, his perpetual smile, his weakness for empty-headed adulators of either sex, or for his outlandish cosmetics and dress. But those who come to know him more than casually may come to be enchanted by his kindness, his accessibility, his ingenuousness and his impeccable manners.

A type

"Aggressive type"

Non-sanguine, non-perfectionistic, aggressive type

A types typically have a non-sanguine complexion, are extroverted, brusque, brash and prone to aggressive arrogance, but not exhibitionistic or narcissistic. The female is sometimes denigrated as "masculine". Circumstances can lead this type to be overtly sadistic. A positive attribute is that he or she gets things done and gets them done fast. Short physical stature is common but not universal.

Rage: Aggressive-vindictive "A rage" (mass discharge of sympathetic nervous system). Also called the "fight or flight" response.

Also known as: Aggressive, choleric personality. "The arrogant dynamo". Non-sanguine autocrat.

Complexion: Non-sanguine. Tending toward pallid or sallow in individuals of light skin color. May be milky white. Does not blush easily.

Smile: Sardonic smirk. Non-gingival, half-open mouthed grin. Grin with short, repetitive laugh to mask the incapacity to smile.

Photograph: Looks at camera. "Pleased-with-self" grin.

Voice: Confident, confrontational, abrasive, bullying.

Gestures: Clenched fist, aggressive finger point, haughtily-cocked jaw, intimidating glare.

Handwriting: Non-perfectionistic. Often slurred or bold illegible scrawl.

Sexuality: Tendency to promiscuity: moderate. Tendency to LGBT in sexual orientation: low-moderate.

Color preference: Inattentive approach to color choice.

Population genetics: "The Militant Habitancy", having a high prevalence of A and PA types. Examples: Yemen, Arab part of Iraq, other Middle Eastern subpopulations.

Susceptibilities: Attention deficit disorders (ADD, ADHD). Overt sadism, sociopathology. Antisocial personality disorder. Explosive rages. Sadomasochistic "morbid dependency" as the dominant partner. Leader of authoritarian, militant or genocidal movement. "Absolute power corrupts absolutely."

Pitfalls: High-temperament PA types can resemble A types. Accounts of the behavior of NA or NPA+ types can resemble A types. An A type, in a drive for power, may mount the podium, leading to mistaken conclusion of the N trait. "Punky" adornment may lead to mistaken conclusion of the N trait (pseudo-narcissism).

Character caricature [7]

He conveys the impression that "I am the strongest. I come first. Period!" He cannot help but be an extrovert and be overtly arrogant. To him arrogance is power, since in arrogating to himself qualities of special importance, nay of omnipotence, he can self-righteously use the brute force of a steamroller to attain his goals. His hallmark is that of seeking the vindictive triumph in overt intimidation, or indeed in any manner that is available to him. He should be able to do anything to anyone, but no one — but no one — can have any claim on him. He is loud. He cannot be missed. He is first.

He "plays the game" of dominance and submission but compulsively must dominate all others. He will avoid at all costs his own subjugation in a personal relationship or in a "morbid dependency"; rather he will be the subjugator. He may split his personality for short periods of time to a subdued state, but will be most unhappy there and will emerge fighting. Having so much invested in aggressive dominance, he will scorn anyone and anything reminiscent of weakness or of submissive tenderness. When opposed, he is the master of vindictive retaliation, and will thirst for the thrill of the vindictive triumph, with strict accountability until retribution is obtained. When attaining subjugation over others he may become sadistic, but his sadism is in the realm of brute force: it is out in the open for all to see. When cornered, with his back to the wall, he will fight and may be at his best.

He has little in the way of narcissistic qualities, hence he has less invested in the anticipation of future accomplishment than in the maintenance of a position of power, where no one can have any claim on him. He has little in the way of perfectionist qualities; therefore, his actions are coarse, with a premium on speedy, goal-oriented, self-obtained satisfaction. He is thus openly hedonistic. Perfectionism by quiet, careful repetitive action is alien to him.

When frustrated, he has in his armamentarium the aggressive-vindictive "A rage", which may be activated with a hair trigger. With repeated defeats he may undergo a depression to an abject state of hopelessness…

His complexion tends to be sallow rather than sanguine. Lacking the sanguine trait, he tends not to adorn himself. But he cannot be missed. He has a loud voice and a brusque demeanor. He is rough around the edges. He is arrogant, aggressive and often cannot help being callous. He is a steamroller who cannot be stopped, or if he is halted, it is only for a moment. He must be first, and no one can have any true claim on him. If he does submit to others, it is he who is magnanimously doing them a favor.

He cuts corners in almost every aspect of his life, in his relations with others, in time, in space, in his poor handwriting and in the realm of the truth. Perfectionist traits of careful, directed activity and of a sense of duty to others are alien to him. He will be happy to say that doing something over and over again to make it better and better will only make it worse and worse. To him it is obvious: perfectionism is the enemy of progress.

He is not by nature a contemplative person; hence, he has only the slightest understanding of the forces that propel him. And it is only for the most fleeting moments of introspection that he wonders why he must so often act like the callous boor that he so often is.

He may not realize it, but his *modus operandi* is a claim of omnipotence. If in his present situation he is not the lord and master, then he tells himself that he soon will be. He "plays the game" of dominance and submission, and to the extent that he considers himself the master of all, his eye contact with others is often poor. Why should he, the all-powerful master, waste his time with eye contact on mere weaklings?

If he is seriously criticized, he will bristle and shoot from the hip. His argumentative reply will not finish until he has achieved a vindictive triumph. He must have the last word.

Just as he does not know how to give thanks or give compliments, he does not know how to apologize. Whatever the issue at hand, truth becomes secondary to an instinctive urge telling him that power must prevail. In fact, in a competitive society he is a dynamo whose meaning, and satisfaction, in life is the vindictive triumph over all individuals, whom in the final analysis he considers to be weaker than he. But satisfaction in life through the vindictive triumph over weaker individuals is, the reader will recall, our definition of sadism, so in the wrong time and the wrong place he is capable not only of the most callous disregard of the rights of others, but also the worst of cruel, sadistic acts.

In better circumstances, his aggressive tendencies are out in the open for all to see. His friends, family and acquaintances will come to recognize and predict his vindictiveness and his accountability for retribution like an elephant that never forgets. They will come to be accustomed to his vindictive rages, much like modern city dwellers become accustomed to the sonic boom. And despite his self-devotion, his hedonism, his arrogance, his brashness and his brusqueness, they may like him. This may be because they have sensed that in admiring him, and in letting him know that they admire him, they give him his only link to tenderness in interpersonal relations: personal recognition for his accomplishments. And they learn that this is the only way to gain his fleeting "smile".

Finally, he may be admired by both the strong and the weak for his qualities of getting things done, and getting them done fast. "Damn the torpedoes! Full steam ahead, come hell or high water!"

As a "player of the game" of dominance and submission, he must be the dominant figure, and so it must be in love relations, which are, of course, usually based on the subjugation of other weaker aggressive or passive aggressive types. And if his daily life is one modest vindictive triumph after another, then his true vindictive rages may be few and far between. He may then be less of an Attila the Hun or a Genghis Khan than a brusque, abrasive dynamo who, despite his being a prisoner of the primeval forces that drive him, charges through life as a useful functioning member of society.

NA type

"Sanguine-aggressive type"

Sanguine, non-perfectionistic, aggressive type

NA types tend to be sanguine-complexioned, hyperactive extroverts. Both traits of ambition, i.e., "unbridled" narcissism and aggression, are fully manifest. NA individuals may be characterized by intemperate behavior not conducive to stable relationships. If the trait of aggression predominates, then the NA type may exhibit sadistic behavior. The NA type often seeks celebrity status, especially in the performing arts.

Rage: Narcissistic "N rage" or aggressive "A rage" or combined "NA rage".

Also known as: "Narcissistic-aggressive type". Cyclothymic, histrionic, hysterical or hypomanic-depressive personality. "The ambitious predator". The *prima donna*.

Complexion: Tending toward sanguine or flushed in individuals of light skin color. NA types have the capacity to blush but typically are unembarrassable.

Smile: Showy, glamorous smile of a movie star.

Photograph: Looks at camera. Extroverted, flashy smile.

Voice: Confident. Highly-modulated with mini-bursts of rapid-fire speech.

Gestures: Active or hyperactive gestures. Often seductive body contact in casual social situations.

Handwriting: Variable, non-perfectionistic. Sometimes rounded, elegant letters in female.

Sexuality: Tendency to promiscuity: high. Tendency to LGBT in sexual orientation: low.

Color preference: Bright yellow, pink, orange, multicolors. Even chartreuse. No particular attraction to red.

Population genetics: "The Corybantic Habitancy", having a high prevalence of NA types. Examples: Brazil, West Africa, indigenous Australia, New Guinea.

Susceptibilities: Attention deficit disorders (ADD, ADHD). Narcissistic personality disorder (NPD). Hysteria, hypochondria, fugues. Hypomanic, histrionic personality. Bipolar disorder. Manic episodes. Explosive rages. Eating disorders. Sadomasochistic "morbid dependency" as the dominant or dependent partner.

Pitfalls: High temperament N types or NPA+ types can resemble NA types. High temperament, zany, pseudo-narcissistic PA types can mimic NA types. A sullen, depressed NA type can resemble a PA type.

Character caricature [7]

He would synergistically combine the mottos, "I am the most glorious" and "I am the most powerful". Thus, lacking the trait of perfectionism, his life is ruled by the unbridled ambition of the traits of narcissism and aggression. We surmise that these two traits, as expressed separately in the N and A personages, would be found together in this individual.

The synergistic drives for both power and glory must produce an extroverted, hyperactive individual. Given the pride invested in "I am beautiful" and "I am powerful", one would expect this individual to be domineering, with an almost megalomanic drive for ambition, in power, glory and sexual domination. This individual lacks concerted perfectionist qualities, hence his search for power and glory is likely to be superficial, spasmodic and lacking in direction.

When reduced to the subdued state NA− this individual strongly resembles the self-flaunting unaggressive sanguine personage N. Of course, he "plays the game" of dominance and submission, and with his hyperactivity and tendency toward hypersexuality he would involve himself in many compulsive dependencies, usually as the subjugator but sometimes as the subjugated individual. As is often the case in such relationships, he may become overtly sadistic, especially in frustrating and in playing on the emotions of his subjugated companions, of which there may be several at one time. And he too, if opposed, seeks retribution in the self-justified vindictive triumph.

This individual when frustrated can be incited to the "N rage" (truly a narcissistic rage), to the "A rage" (truly an aggressive rage), or to a combined narcissistic-aggressive "NA rage". In the latter, the aggressive-vindictive component usually appears first, followed by the narcissistic rage of withdrawal as the individual leaves, slamming the door behind him...

This individual is driven by the unbridled instincts of narcissism and aggression, without mediation of these traits by that of perfectionism. Thus, the behavioral qualities found in the N and A types presented previously may also appear in essentially unaltered form in the NA individual.

This individual is an extrovert, there is no question about that. He usually has a moderately loud voice, but more than loud he is talkative, or outright loquacious. His loquacity is characterized by bursts of rapid speech and has a gossipy quality to it, often with the use of slang expressions, sexual innuendo, and many references to current fads. He is vivacious, flamboyant, flashy, theatrical and somewhat agitated. He may have a hyperactive, labile, mercurial quality and may employ openly seductive body language, accompanied by agitated gestures. He may be in a state of perpetual motion, literally being unable to sit still. Others may comment that "He runs around like a chicken with his head cut off". We might say that he has flounce and he has bounce.

He may be described as charming, but his charm seems to lack any real depth, as if it were a highly-polished artificial veneer. He seems in posture and in manner to be self-assured, but his self-assurance, like his other qualities, seems to be superficial, as if it could be popped like a balloon. In the same way, he may be described as attractive, but more in the literal sense of being capable of attracting the opposite sex, rather than having the attributes of profound beauty. He does not hesitate to talk about any subject, in public or in private, with little regard as to whether it might cause embarrassment to his companion in conversation. In fact, he is practically unembarrassable. He may be "nosey". To use American parlance, "he has a lot of verve and a lot of nerve".

With his agitation and vibrancy, his eye contact with others is often not good, and this is, once more, true to the extent that he feels himself to be above others. His laugh may be loud, penetrating and in the female shrill, but may seem to be forced. He smiles easily. The female can, with especial ease, flash a charming smile at will and hold it indefinitely, as if for a photograph.

As was true for the A type, he is basically aggressive and must dominate over all others, in little matters and in big, in every way and throughout every day. If challenged, or even if not challenged, he may be arrogant, brash and belligerent. If a stressed relationship is to be terminated, whether with a friend, a colleague, an acquaintance or a mate, it must be terminated in the context of a vindictive triumph. And the snarling, vicious, directed vindictive rage is certainly in his repertoire but may rarely be seen.

In his perpetual motion he fills up his time with trips, visits, classes and activities but is not really a "workaholic" in the sense of devoting himself to any real work. He is a dilettante. He is at his best in task-oriented activities. He tends to lack any deep sense of duty. Lacking in perfectionist qualities, he has little staying power. His most reliable attributes are his impulsiveness and his inconstancy.

He is, if you listen to him, intensely ambitious and he may say so in those words, but there is a great discrepancy between his ambitions and his real accomplishments. Sometimes he seems propelled by the jet stream of his own self-generated hot air. He is extravagant. There is a definite proclivity to travel, preferably by airplane, and it seems as if someone else is always paying for his trip. He is an intensely social person, a partygoer, and indeed the classic "life of the party". And as he becomes older, lacking the staying power for satisfying his deep needs for accomplishment and affection, he senses that something is wrong, that perhaps he is not "normal". But more often than not, he will acknowledge that of course he is not normal — he is exceptional!

His relations with the opposite sex may be characterized as troublesome, turbulent and tormenting. Although the range of variability in human behavior in the realm of sexuality is enormously wide, there is no question that many of these individuals place a premium on sexuality in their lives. Some of them could well be placed into the bygone categories of satyriasis and nymphomania. He is a coquette, a tease, a bird of prey, a vampire. There may be a continual, compulsive search for sexual partners, ostensibly to satisfy a conscious desire for a stable relationship. Instead, there occurs only one turbulent, tormenting relationship after another, and he views the past in perplexed amazement as he recounts how many partners fell in love with him, how many wanted to marry him, and how many he crushed by leaving them abruptly…

Finally, we reiterate the wide range of emotional behavior of the NA type: his hypomanic highs and his abject depressive lows. He may be prone to obesity as he alternately overeats in splurges and then abstains from food entirely. He is particularly prone to psychosomatic illness, for example to headaches, intestinal problems, palpitations, or attacks of "nervousness"…

When intimidated he may split his personality abruptly to the NA− subdued state, where he becomes a narcissistic type with not a trace of aggression to be seen…

Finally, if we add to the NA individual's behavioral repertoire the occurrence of the combined narcissistic-aggressive NA rage, we see the extent to which this individual is a captive of his emotions.

NP type

"Sanguine-perfectionistic type"

Sanguine, perfectionistic, non-aggressive type

NP types are usually reserved, unaggressive individuals, tending toward a sanguine complexion and a propensity to blush easily. The N trait of sanguinity is "bridled" by the P trait, so overt narcissism is absent. This is the dutiful, aloof individual who is obsessive and compulsive with regard to order, symmetry and neatness. Despite being unaggressive, these individuals can be very stubborn. Low temperament individuals may be described as "melancholic", while high temperament individuals can be "nervous birds" and may be more sociable. Tall and lean physical stature is common but not universal.

Rage: Narcissistic "N rage".

Also known as: "Narcissistic-perfectionist type". Obsessive-compulsive personality. Phlegmatic-melancholic or bovine personality. "Nervous bird" personality. "The aloof achiever".

Complexion: Tending toward sanguine or flushed in individuals of light skin color. Prone to blush very easily.

Smile: Uncommon sudden warm, radiant sheepish smile. Sometimes gingival smile (broadly exposing gums and teeth). The gingival smile is striking when seen, but may be rare, especially in melancholic individuals.

Photograph: Looks at camera. Relaxed face; sheepish, sometimes radiant "limelight" smile.

Voice: Confident, measured, deferential.

Gestures: Sometimes "narcissistic arms" gesture in which the arms are extended in front of the individual, with palms up and the fingers somewhat spread apart. It is a pose often assumed by singers and by religious leaders when praising their gods.

Handwriting: Almost invariably well-formed, with each letter clearly legible. Sometimes striking calligraphic quality. Sometimes tiny, well-formed letters.

Sexuality: Tendency to promiscuity: very low. Tendency to LGBT in sexual orientation: very low.

Color preference: Subdued colors. Dark blue, black, white, black-and-white, beige. Tends to avoid bright red, especially in female.

Population genetics: "The Punctilious Habitancy", having a high prevalence of NP types and very few A or PA types. Examples: Switzerland, Germany, Scandinavia, Taiwan.

Susceptibilities: Obsessive-compulsive personality disorder (OCPD). Narcissistic personality disorder (NPD, may be masked by individual's perfectionist trait). Tantrums. "Control freak". Hoarding disorder. Unipolar, postpartum depression. Compulsive criminal. Autism or Asperger syndrome. Epilepsy. Leukemia. Rheumatic and congenital heart disease. CVA (stroke). Down's syndrome parent.

Pitfalls: Can be mistaken for a perfectionistic PA type or Passive Aggressive NPA− or NPA= type. High temperament individuals can superficially resemble NPA+ types. An NP type in a position of authority can be a rigid disciplinarian, meting out severe punishment (pseudo-aggression). The compulsive need for "control" may be misinterpreted as the "thirst for power". In imminent psychosis, the hyperactive behavior of an NP type can mimic aggressive behavior.

Character caricature [7]

This individual has narcissistic qualities that are mediated by the trait of perfectionism. Thus, he has narcissistic ambition ("I will be glorious") but also perfectionistic qualities ("Do it well..."). This individual would be well motivated, but a perfectionist plodder. He would be slow. He would do it over and over again. He would chip away at something ever so slowly, so he will not go too fast, or too far all at once. He must be something of a loner. He must be somewhat subdued. He fills up his time with activities, doing, redoing, starting, not quite finishing, polishing, giving him a "workaholic" quality. His time may be filled with ambitious goals, but slow repetitive actions, so that he is always late for appointments. We propose that he may be one of the so-called obsessive-compulsive individuals of the psychiatric literature.

He has his eye on the limelight, to be sure, with a vision toward the future. But the self-flaunting aspect of the previously described narcissistic N type is mediated by this individual's necessity to be perfect in all ways. Thus, the conceit of the narcissistic individual is moderated into persistent achievement in quiet modesty. In fact, this individual feels that he must do whatever his friends, family and society demand of him as a perfect person. He simply must try to do to the best of his ability what he feels he should do. And he feels that he should do everything. And do it perfectly. Thus, to his friends, to his family and to himself, he is a prisoner of his own sense of duty. He is a quiet achiever but at the same time a prisoner of perfection.

Although the traits of sanguinity and perfectionism appear to be acting in concert, it is apparent that the demands of modern society can lead to great conflicts in this character type. Narcissism gives him the vision of a glorious future and the possibility of the limelight, while perfectionism is the root of his excruciating, painstakingly slow progress. In addition, no human being can possibly accomplish in the time of twenty-four hours all that he expects of himself, not to mention all the demands that others place on him.

Lacking aggressive qualities, he is defenseless against aggressive types. He does not "play the game" of dominance and submission, does not split his personality to a subdued state, and cannot be induced into an aggressive-vindictive rage. He is not sexually aggressive in a predatory manner. Since his love relations cannot be based on a dominant-submissive relationship, he loves on the basis of his narcissistic and perfectionist qualities. In particular, he loves because he should love, and he is tender because he should be tender. In fact, he will do anything that a devoted mate should do, simply because his inner nature tells him, "I deserve it to myself and to everyone that I should do everything perfectly."

In essence, his attitude in its compulsive rigidity becomes equivalent to a "deal with life". If he pays attention to all the details of life, if everything is neatly in its place, if he has thought of everything in advance, then nothing should go wrong. And when things do go wrong, whether they are by any stretch of the imagination his fault or not, he blames himself for not having foreseen the difficulty. This may send him to the doldrums of a melancholic abject state for days or months, especially if the cause of the failure actually was some deficiency on his part.

He may be incited to the perfectionistic-narcissistic rage when frustrated by others. This begins as a few moments of inwardly directed seething, and then may break out into an agitated narcissistic "N rage" of defense and withdrawal.

Finally, we note that in the NP character structure we expect to find a quiet, unaggressive individual who should be content with perfecting the various aspects of his life with a minimum of conflict with others. However, in a poorly adjusted individual his inner voices may demand of him an incessant repetition of bizarre acts, so that he may attempt to satisfy some poorly-understood need for order or completeness in his life. If these acts come into conflict with the norms of his society, then he may become a compulsive gambler or bank robber, a kleptomanic collector, or even a ritualistic murderer. Hence, such an individual, although lacking the aggressive behavioral trait, could certainly be branded as "aggressive" by his society...

We will describe the NP type with the understanding that the baseline temperament of these individuals may vary widely, from the "phlegmatic" to the "nervous".

If one were required to describe this individual as an introvert or extrovert, one would tend to say that he is a quiet, friendly, sincere, somewhat sheepish introvert. He is polite, dependable, calm, careful, conscientious, considerate and cooperative. He is modest, pleasant and cheerfully reserved. He may have a pensive, bashful quality. He is unselfish, tolerant and sympathetic. He is neat and scrupulously attentive to detail. His desk is usually neat, his affairs are in order, and his dress, although not necessarily fashionable, is impeccable. He does not have an unbridled need to adorn himself. He may have a fetish for order, symmetry, neatness, with a place for everything and everything in its place. His handwriting is usually highly legible, with every letter clearly visible. It may have a calligraphic quality. A piece of work imperfectly done or lying unfinished causes him no end of smoldering grief. He may be a compulsive house cleaner.

He has a strong sense of duty: dutifulness to his family, to his friends, to his country, perhaps to his god, and to himself. In his duty to himself he must accomplish what he must, and this may sometimes be one detailed task after another. Thus, he may develop a "workaholic" quality to his life, always seemingly busy and always late. He may be a contemplative procrastinator. He is, therefore, punctilious but not necessarily punctual.

He is almost universally liked, or regarded to be a quiet person who is benignly tolerated. In American parlance, he is often a "nice guy" or a "fine gal". He may be somewhat prudish or even pious. He seems to be rather aloof, ignoring others in a benign way as he quietly goes about his business of pursuits for his own self-satisfaction. However, he is easily approachable and almost always tries to be helpful. He may present himself as a straightforward, uncomplicated person, even a "Simple Simon", but this is misleading and it is only on closer examination that we see the stringent demands that he places on himself.

His natural facial expression is a poker face or deadpan look of perfectionist restraint. As he plays his game of cards, he holds them close to his chest, and he does not particularly wish to discuss how his game is proceeding. In fact, he secretly has everything invested in the finality of success and in the recognition of his success by others. Thus, if recognition does come in any shape or form, whether it is a colleague to bring him good cheer, or actual recognition for something well done in an actual limelight, then he will smile. And his gingival smile, whenever it breaks out through his poker-faced visage, is a sight to behold! It is a warm, radiant, captivating smile, a kind of sheepish smile, appearing suddenly like the sun breaking through the clouds, or of a Cheshire cat suddenly appearing in the mist. It is often so breathtakingly, sincerely radiant that one is led to believe that this smile by itself is enough to give the human race its redeeming social value. And it does not take much insight to realize that this smile is the smile of narcissism bursting forth through the clouds of perfectionism.

As the quiet, somewhat bashful person that he sometimes is, he may surprise others when he mounts the podium as a public speaker. Somewhat stilted at the outset, he slowly gathers momentum and may gradually become radiantly charismatic, especially if he is attempting to persuade his audience.

This individual may have so much pride invested in the recognition of his work as a "conscientious achiever", that embarrassment in the limelight is of special sensitivity to him. In fact, of all the character types, he is the one to blush the most readily. Indeed, in Western society he sometimes has a pinkish or ruddy complexion. If he is male and of the appropriate body habitus, he may have a cherubic, "blushing boy" quality.

He may be quietly ambitious, but lacking qualities of the trait of aggression, this individual is unaggressive and unassertive. He may, in fact, become annoyed when others continually point this out to him. If he is in a position where he should be aggressive, for example as a baseball manager or football coach, he may sometimes adopt a loud voice, but on close inspection he is simply an unaggressive person with a loud voice. Perhaps the most aggressive act of which he is capable is to interrupt someone while he is speaking.

Being unassertive, he finds it difficult to give clear-cut orders. Rather he expects that others will know what to do by his excellent example. He goes forth, and he expects others to follow. But, of course, as they often do not, he may have serious problems maintaining discipline. He cannot berate a subordinate, and he is the master of the short, two-sentence reprimand delivered in an almost apologetic manner.

He does not "play the game" of dominance and submission. His eye contact with others is almost universally good, but does not have the intensity of the NPA+ type. His gestures are reserved, as is his language. Ostentatious behavior is alien to him. His laugh, even if loud, is reserved. His humor has a pleasant impish or elfish quality to it, and he is not the type to play practical jokes of the kind that might cause someone physical discomfort or harm. He enjoys social situations, but is somewhat stilted in demeanor in them.

This usually quiet, unaggressive individual easily bends to the will of others, right? Wrong! He is persistent. He is obstinate. He is recalcitrant. He is downright stubborn! He has a will all of his own, and if he wants to do something in his own orderly way, then wild horses will not be able to budge him from his position.

When criticized he will immediately, quietly, and logically defend his position. If abused, he may scowl, but he may often turn the other cheek, simply not being able to defend himself against aggressive behavior. His only defense may be recalcitrance in the face of the demands of others. He will withdraw himself from the offending individual and ignore him. He will give him "the silent treatment" or pretend not to understand his wishes. He may use various modes of passive resistance, or make lame excuses for his recalcitrance. If pressed further he may quarrel, even vigorously, but he will not fight unless he is cornered. If he does, at long last, punch someone in the nose, it will be in the context of escape or of a narcissistic rage of vanity rather than an aggressive rage of vindictiveness.

He may appear as a somewhat negativistic "passive resister" or "chronic criticizer". If his sense of order is intruded upon repeatedly, he may become more and more negativistic and more and more recalcitrant to the point of resemblance to a PA type. Under greater stress, his negativistic recalcitrance can degenerate either into a catatonic state of near immobility or into a harried nervous state of agitation. In such a latter state he may closely resemble the non-compliant Passive Aggressive NPA− type, or even a hypomanic NA type.

He tends to suffer in silence and to be self-berating. He tends not to be vindictive, neither in a vindictive rage nor in calculated vindictiveness, nor even in frustrating others or begrudging them what is their due. He holds no grudges and sometimes appears to have infinite patience and understanding. He may tease others good-naturedly, even persistently, but this is probably a Western cultural habit, and he is essentially devoid of sadistic trends. If his vanity or his pride in perfection is wounded, then he may respond in a narcissistic "N rage" as has been described earlier.

He is often drawn to activities in which painstaking, repetitive action is required. He may be an artist, a musician, a poet, a craftsman, a collector, or a do-it-yourself tinkerer. He is often the dutiful writer of long, careful letters to his family and he may keep a diary.

In the context of mating, the NP type is not aggressive or predatory, although he will certainly acknowledge that he is a sexual being. If he is promiscuous, the overtones of aggression or exploitation are absent. The subjugated love of the aggressive type is unknown to him, as is sadomasochistic sexuality. His love relations are based on his narcissistic and perfectionist qualities: his love is tender rather than unabashedly passionate. He tends not to "fall in love" easily because the decision to devote himself to a mate must be a perfect decision, and like all of his decisions, is not easily made on the spur of the moment. If he enters into a long-term relation with an aggressive-vindictive personage, for example with an NA type, he may suffer in silence like a "brave wife" or a "henpecked husband", all the while berating himself for not being perfect enough to make the relationship an ideal one.

Finally, in his deal with life: "I will be perfect, so life will be perfect to me" he is especially vulnerable to any failure intruding into his existence, whether it be a flat tire on his automobile, a natural disaster or the loss of a loved one. Such failures may register not only as deep disappointments, but as hopeless reversals in what he perceives should be a natural order in life. The loss of a loved one, in particular of a family member, is an incomprehensible, unbearable crushing blow to him. If he does not throw himself on the pyre, then he will enter a melancholic abject state of deep mourning. He will wear black, literally or figuratively, for months or years and often will take his grief to the grave.

PA type

"Perfectionist-aggressive type"

Non-sanguine, perfectionistic, aggressive type

PA types tend to a non-sanguine complexion. Individuals of low temperament can be well-adjusted stodgy, dutiful, socially conscious "solid citizens". Higher temperament individuals can be somewhat stern or haughty extroverts. If the PA type comes to absolute power, then overt sadistic trends may come to the fore. The PA type is relatively uncommon in the USA and Western Europe but common in the Middle East, Eastern Europe and western Russia.

Rage: Aggressive "A rage".

Also known as: Reserved aggressive personality. Austere melancholic or paranoid personality. Pseudo-narcissistic extrovert. "The sardonic wit". "The suspicious manipulator". "The Power behind the throne".

Complexion: Non-sanguine. Tending toward sallow, pallid or milky white in individuals with light skin color. Does not blush easily.

Smile: Non-symmetric grin or grimace. Mona Lisa "smile". Sardonic smirk. Frozen, toothy but non-gingival grin. Half open-mouthed grin. Grin with short repetitive laugh.

Photograph: Usually looks at camera. May pompously look away from camera. Not relaxed. No smile, half smile, tight-lipped sardonic smile, non-symmetric grin or grimace. Laughs or tries to laugh, showing expressive extroverted countenance.

Voice: Confident, contentious, measured, dispassionate.

Gestures: Upraised clenched fist, the haughtily cocked jaw, the furrowed brow, the strained tight-lipped mouth and the intimidating glare.

Handwriting: Variable. Usually perfectionistic in female. Often slurred or bold illegible scrawl in males. Sometimes bold flourishes or messy corrections.

Sexuality: Tendency to promiscuity: moderate. Tendency to LGBT in sexual orientation: moderate.

Color preference: Conservative, even drab color choices: Muted colors, blue, dark or white. Aversion to red, bright colors and multicolors.

Population genetics: "The Authoritarian Habitancy", having a high prevalence of PA types, moderate prevalence of A and NPA types, and few N and NP types. Examples: Eastern Europe, Balkans.

Susceptibilities: Obsessive paranoia. Paranoid personality disorder. Covert sadism. Sadomasochistic "morbid dependency" as the dominant or dependent partner. "Power behind the throne".

Pitfalls: High temperament PA types can mimic non-sanguine A types, or even NA types. Disciplinarian NP types can resemble PA types. Punky adornment may lead to mistaken conclusion of the N trait (pseudo-narcissism).

Character caricature [7]

Here we have an individual who attempts to streamline both his aggressive and perfectionistic qualities into a cohesive unity. How can he possibly do this? His aggressive behavioral trait tells him to forge ahead, to gain power over all others, to achieve vindictive triumph after triumph, to intimidate, and to be first. However, from the trait of perfectionism comes the subliminal voice, "Do it carefully, slowly, perfectly." Thus, perfectionism pacifies aggression, and here we realize that we have discovered the "passive-aggressive" personality of the psychiatric literature. However, this character is not so much passive-aggressive as perfectionist-aggressive.

In a life situation where he has attained a relative equilibrium, or has achieved success in circumstances where he is not threatened, this type may appear as a quiet or fairly outgoing, well-mannered, somewhat stern individual. He may, like all other types, go through life uneventfully, although his relationships with others may be rather tenuous and distant. He may appear as a relatively content, careful, reliable worker who is persistent and pays attention to detail.

This individual, despite his basic passive-aggressive tendencies, may feel a strong need to interact with people, according to the dictates of the gregariousness that modern society demands of him. He may find himself, in fact, in a life situation where he is constantly interacting with others in more or less stressful circumstances. He may then appear in one of two different forms. In one form, he is an individual who sees himself as a perfectionist worker, but whose aspirations are constantly being thwarted by the imperfections or malevolence of others. He, thus, becomes the "chronic complainer" or "chronic criticizer". In a second form, he appears as a fairly gregarious individual with a cutting, sarcastic sense of humor: the "sardonic wit".

If this individual aspires to high ambition, his lack of the N trait means that his ambition must be vested entirely in his aggressive drive. Since his perfectionist trait does not permit the overt use of force, he must use it quietly, unobtrusively, insidiously, obstructively. To a casual observer it may not be noticeably visible. He becomes a manipulator, quietly accumulating relevant information, pondering over it, collating it, putting it into place, using it for insidious, obstructive attacks on others and using it to batten his defensive perimeter. As he becomes manipulative, he becomes more and more mistrustful of others, including his superiors, his colleagues and his subordinates. And in the general mistrust of others he becomes suspicious, cynical and paranoid. Hence, we believe that any study of the paranoid personality type might begin with the study of this character structure.

On a personal level, the PA type, of course, "plays the game" of dominance and submission, becomes involved in subjugation dependencies, and is subject to incitement from a quiet state to the perfectionist-aggressive rage. This begins as a period of outwardly directed seething, and then with the slightest provocation bursts into a directed aggressive-vindictive "A rage".

When dominated, this individual enters a subdued PA− state of perfectionistic schizoid behavior. Thus, he must attempt at all costs to maintain a position of dominance. If, however, he is dislodged from his position, and hopelessness sets in, then he is subject to a deep abject state of schizoid depression...

As with all the character types, the PA type includes a wide spectrum of individuals who may be enormously successful, and greatly admired, in their societies.

With regard to the physiognomy of the PA individual, his complexion tends to be dull rather than sanguine. It is often swarthy, pale, pallid, dusky or sallow. In a fair individual it may be milky white. His countenance is usually one of a deadpan poker face. In his choice of dress and cosmetics he tends not to adorn himself in an outlandish manner. He may present himself as a "strong silent type", exhibiting courteous reserved charm and well-mannered gallantry. Thus, in unstressed circumstances he may have the quiet personal magnetism of the NP type. He may be greatly admired for his proud bearing, his undemonstrative low-key manner, and his dry humor, often providing others a welcome relief from the madding hysteria of modern society.

The individual of this character type may present himself as something of a high-strung extrovert. More often than not, he tends to keep to himself and may lead a fairly quiet life as a somewhat wary, withdrawn but coolly efficient perfectionist achiever. But with his aggressive drive frustrated to a muted level by the trait of perfectionism, what may emerge is a laconic individual who displays an imperfectly concealed deep dissatisfaction with life. This will not go unnoticed, and his acquaintances will sometimes accuse him, behind his back, of having an air of haughty superiority.

If this individual is constantly interacting with others in a fairly competitive or stressful setting, he may become the classic "passive-aggressive" obstructionist personality, who will not accede to the desires of others except in the most grudging manner. If he is a bit more of an extrovert, then he too may appear as a "chronic complainer" or "chronic criticizer".

Alternatively, this moody personage may find that an effective link with humanity can be made only through the medium of dry humor. In this case, he appears in public as something of a gregarious individual who relies, compulsively and almost exclusively, on his "sardonic wit" to gain the favor of others. Such an individual may display a real talent for creative, albeit sarcastic, humor, and he may be immensely popular with his colleagues for this quality.

In the description that follows, we will present a caricature of one particular PA subtype when he is thrown into the throes of a stressful competitive society, into a position of leadership, or when he is involved in a love relationship.

When this individual is encountered in a stressful setting, one finds oneself picturing him alternately as either an introvert or extrovert. Basically, he appears as a moody extrovert in whom one senses an undercurrent of deep hostility toward the outside world.

He tends to isolate himself, to be introspective and to be basically unfriendly. He is usually coldly calm, but when he is involved in a stressful ambitious venture, a directed task, or a situation of conflict with people, he may become mildly or severely agitated. His pallid face will blanch even more. His normally even voice will rise and have a cutting quality to it. It may barely hide a snarl. His eyes will flash and his brow will furrow. And in his voice one senses not only anger, but also the contempt and disdain of others, and a thinly veiled threat of vindictiveness.

His face in calmer circumstances usually shows the deadpan look of an austere poker-faced perfectionist. Although he is usually at ease before a group of people, to the extent that he believes that he dominates over them, he does not smile easily. What usually emerges is an odd grimace or a grin. He is usually aware of the fact that he cannot at will break out into a natural smile, and in compensation he has developed a short, repetitive laugh accompanied by a closed or half-open mouthed grin, which for him takes the place of the smile that his modern society demands of him. If he tries to smile for a photograph, the result is usually a broad "false smile", a non-symmetric frozen grin, or a sardonic smirk, and often he will not even try.

His handwriting may reflect either his perfectionist or aggressive tendencies. The handwriting may be neat and well formed, especially in the female. In contrast, it may be a slurred illegible scrawl, signifying at the same time his instincts of repressed physical aggression and his disdain for others.

In relations with people he pictures himself as a superior person and would not see himself as isolated. However, his view of life may be seen by his usual physical posture, which is sometimes slightly stooped, with the head dropped slightly down and his eyes directed to the ground before him. He may have, in fact, an amazing capacity to ignore people around him in familiar surroundings, almost to the point of obliviousness. When encountering a subordinate, or in a social setting, his normally stooped posture may change to one of erect, pompous rigidity. His basic unfriendliness may be reflected in obligatory but only cursory greetings to acquaintances or colleagues.

In a stressful social situation where strangers are present he gives the impression of being decidedly uncomfortable and will adopt either a posture of defensive rigidity or will be somewhat agitated. When meeting people in public, he has the roving eyes of suspiciousness, as if scanning the horizon for the possible approach of enemy aircraft. He instinctively evaluates a new arrival for his strengths and weaknesses, as his eyes move in frequent saccades of critical examination. What he is looking for, of course, is the new arrival's particular weakness, his soft underbelly, for in his isolation he senses himself vulnerable, and the only way to conquer his vulnerability is to dominate all others and to be stronger than them.

To the extent that he feels above his fellow humans, he does not make good eye contact with them. If challenged, however, he is the master of staring down his opponent to submission with a steely-eyed intimidating glare or glower. It is a glower that says, "You had better do what I, the perfectionist, expect, or else my vindictive rage may be activated with a hair trigger." His general demeanor, then, may be austere and dour, and may have a sinister aspect to it. His lips may take the form of a fixed smirk. He is the past master of the short derisive laugh.

Is he sarcastic and pessimistic? Yes, he certainly is. But he may be more than that. He may be deeply cynical, and one senses that behind the cynicism of the disasters to come lies the wish for a self-fulfilling prophecy. And in his cynicism and his brooding nature, which exudes the gloom of the basic hopelessness of the human condition, we find the roots of his defensive paranoia and his offensive sadistic potential.

In a position of power, being aloof and suspicious, he is almost unapproachable to his subordinates or colleagues. His door is usually closed, and telephone calls are made in an atmosphere of secretiveness and suspicion. To the extent that he is secretive and mistrustful of others, so are others mistrustful of him. And if they do not trust him, they are intimidated by him, and they are ill at ease with him.

He is an individual who is above all self-righteous, and absolutely convinced that his position of dominance over others is not only right, but inevitable. He may develop a sense of invulnerability. When the going gets tough, and the weaklings scatter in all directions, he will stand firm, tall and proud, with his back to the wall if necessary, and he will survive over, nay conquer, all of his adversaries.

Is he a perfectionist? Yes, he certainly is. He has a sense of duty, but he lacks a broader sense of devotion to others that is often present in the NP and NPA types. His perfectionism lies in the area of pacifying his aggressive tendencies, so that they operate smoothly with maximum efficiency, which means that they are insidious and almost unseen. His *modus operandi* may be summarized by the expression "manipulation with care".

As he discovers, consciously or unconsciously, that his relationships with people are distant, he may attempt to invert his aloofness from time to time. As a perfectionist, an inner voice tells him that he should be warm, loving, sympathetic and gregarious. He will, then, from time to time descend to the level of the lower minions to mingle with his subordinates and colleagues, banter with them, "smile" with them, and attempt to prove to them, and to himself, that at the core he is a down-to-earth humane person. And he must, almost invariably, have at least one "exception that proves the rule" in a cause, or in a person to whom he shows, openly, care and devotion.

He, of course, "plays the game" of dominance and submission, and here we will only briefly mention the implications of this tendency rooted in his aggressive drives. If he is subjugated in marriage or in a love relationship, then he may find himself in a helpless schizoid state and may be reduced to achieving dominance only in occasional vindictive rages. In the dominant role he is, of course, much more successful, provided that his partner is not completely helpless or too tolerant of abuse. Finally, his love relationship may assume a stable symbiotic form in which he adopts the role of what we call the "power behind the throne". As the "power" he protects his mate, who is his sole source of security in life, with all the perfectionist-aggressive talent that his personality type can muster. This type of relationship, the dynamics of which are not consciously perceived by either individual, is discussed in detail elsewhere [7].

It goes without saying that a motivated PA type is no less committed to success in life through the vindictive triumph over others than is the aggressive A type. The difference lies in the muted way that he goes about it: by manipulation, by conniving, by holding grudges, by begrudging others amenities that they desire or recognition that they deserve, by withholding information from them, and in short, by an always ongoing process of perfecting a multitude of interrelated offensive and defensive actions, so that the final result is a fine tapestry of interwoven vindictive triumphs.

As is the case with all of the personages, this type is one who arouses pathos, for he too is a prisoner of his character structure. He is a prisoner of his aggressive tendencies, for if they were to be suppressed he would be left with only an aimless perfectionistic drive, with no ambition to perfect, and he would thus become schizoid and immobile.

NPA type

"Sanguine-perfectionistic-aggressive type"

NPA types tend to be sanguine-complexioned, overbearing maternalistic or paternalistic extroverts. All three of the NPA traits are present and fully expressed. Exhibitionism and overt narcissism may be tempered by the P trait. The voice is LOUD and the eye contact intense. NPA types tend to be conventional in their dress and behavior. Their greatest vulnerability is the tendency to explosive rages, often followed by forced affability or apologetics. The female is sometimes denigrated as being "masculine".

The Dominant NPA type is sometimes denoted as *NPA+* for clarity.

Rage: Narcissistic "N rage" or aggressive "A rage" or combined "NPA rage".

Also known as: "Narcissistic-perfectionistic-aggressive type". Explosive personality. Managerial-autocratic personality. "The overbearing achiever". The sanguine autocratic tyrant.

Complexion: Tending toward sanguine or flushed in individuals of light skin color, especially when agitated.

Smile: Warm paternalistic or maternalistic smile.

Photograph: Looks at camera. Relaxed smile.

Voice: Very loud, intense, modulated. Non-stop garrulous. Pontificating.

Gestures: Active or hyperactive gestures. Intense eye contact with loud, penetrating voice. Often non-seductive body contact in casual social situations.

Handwriting: Variable. Often perfectionistic but sometimes grossly illegible.

Sexuality: Tendency to promiscuity: low. Tendency to LGBT in sexual orientation: very low.

Color preference: Rather conservative in color choice, as opposed to the more flamboyant color choices of the NA type.

Population genetics: "The Demonstrative Habitancy", having a high prevalence of NPA and NA types. Examples: Mediterranean subpopulations, Colombia.

Susceptibilities: Overbearing need for control. Explosive personality disorder. Megalomania. Narcissistic personality disorder (NPD).

Pitfalls: In absolute power the NPA type can be a cruel disciplinarian, resembling the behavior of an A type. Hyperactive, high-temperament NPA types can resemble NA types. Loud N types (especially male) can be confused with NPA types. For short duration, a Passive Aggressive NPA– type can mimic an NPA type.

Character caricature [7]

This individual obviously has a concurrent combination of all three of the NPA behavioral traits: glory, perfection and power. We would expect the following qualities: narcissistic ambition, perfectionistic attention to detail and sense of duty, and the aggressive need for triumph through power. It is not difficult to surmise that this person would be outgoing, active, and vigorous.

This individual, having aggressive qualities, "plays the game" of dominance and submission, splits his personality to a subdued NPA– state when dominated. His love is based on his narcissistic qualities, on the dynamics of the dependency of subjugation, as well as on his sense of perfectionist duty.

This character type would be the most susceptible to be incited to rages, since both his vanity based on narcissism and his pride based on omnipotence are subject to being wounded. This is the narcissistic-perfectionistic-aggressive super-rage, or "NPA rage". This often begins with some violation, reasonable or not, of the individual's sense of perfection, order or justice. That is, all rules should be followed exactly; everything should be exactly in its place. After a few milliseconds of seething, an explosive rage bursts forth, first having an aggressive-vindictive quality to it and being personally directed. Gradually it becomes directed to the horizon, and may finally end as a narcissistic rage of defense and withdrawal. After the rage subsides, this individual's sense of duty may require him to apologize...

There is no question about it. He is an extrovert. His complexion definitely tends toward the sanguine, especially if he is at all agitated. His voice has an unrestrained quality. It may be forceful. In the female it may have a sharp, piercing quality. His voice may be outright loud, even if he consciously tries not to be overbearing, which often he is. His voice may be very, very LOUD. It may be stentorian, especially in the male, and he may sometimes be heard at the far end of a railway car. It is a voice that seems to long for diffuse dissemination, as he speaks at and through his partner in conversation. It is a voice of narcissism ("how grand I am") and of aggression ("all of you had better listen to what I am saying"). Often he can be identified immediately by his forceful voice alone.

This individual is not relaxed. He radiates a certain intensity and activity, and like the NA type, he too may have difficulty keeping still. In manner, he may be only moderately outgoing, especially if he is in circumstances where he is chronically dominated by stronger individuals. On the other hand, he may be intensely outgoing, affably ebullient or outright truculent. If he is only moderately intense, he has a certain amount of real charm, but often he is so frankly overbearing that his charm is lost in his abrasiveness. He is never at a loss for words. At times he may talk, and talk... and talk. And in his garrulity his smile and laughter may take on a forced intensity.

He has a moderate gait and carries himself with relative confidence. This individual seems to be going somewhere. He usually makes intense eye contact with his partner in conversation, whether the latter be strong or weak, important or unimportant. His prominent eyes have a spirited look about them and may seem to sparkle or even protrude.

In the mature adult, he has a non-seductive maternalistic or paternalistic character, even if he is promiscuous. In the female, she has more of a "wholesome" than a "sexy" demeanor. If her voice is very forceful, her detractors will say that she is "not feminine," "brassy" or even "masculine".

He is reliable, dependable and responsible. He is faithful to his family and friends. If he has children, he has affectionate pride in them and talks about them. He is a "solid citizen". He has a sense of duty to his profession, his colleagues, his business, perhaps his church, and his country. He tends to have a sense of citizenship, of attachments, and of devotion to some ideals. He is, shall we say... rather conventional.

He is expansive, something of a perfectionist and a "doer". His perfectionist tendencies are not as constraining as in the NP type, and he actually gets things done. He likes to get the present job finished and move on to the next task, and he may be a true "workaholic", with his time filled with real activities. Although he may be a procrastinator, he dislikes intensely any ambiguous situations, incomplete information, work half-finished, or any feeling of "loose strings hanging". He tends to be impatient and sometimes impetuous. He cannot bear to stand and watch someone doing something slowly or fumbling about, and will immediately say, "Here, let me do it for you."

We usually see in him a person who is cordial, but who has an air of self-importance. And it is in this feeling of self-importance that there may emerge a barely concealed attitude of callousness, for example in being late for appointments or in downgrading the wishes and aspirations of others.

His gestures are expansive. He may have friendly body contact with his colleagues and acquaintances, but in contrast to that of the NA type, it is of a non-seductive nature. His clothes are usually fitting for the occasion, but he is not one to devote himself to superficial fads or fashions. In the male, especially, his shoes will be polished and his hair combed, but his clothes may even be somewhat ill-fitting. He is, thus, more properly dressed than truly fashionably or gaudily dressed. To the extent that narcissistic-perfectionist tendencies predominate, which is often the case, he will make an effort to have clear, legible handwriting, even when he is in a hurry.

In social situations, he may be at his best. He is the classic after-dinner speaker. He may be a master of inverted modesty in speaking before an audience (e.g., "*He* is an absolutely fantastic person"). He indulges in "hail-fellow-well-met". At a social function he may bellow across the crowded room to welcome a prestigious individual when the latter arrives. He is sympathetic at the core, from his sense of duty, but does not tend to spout forth spontaneous sentimental affection.

If someone does not uphold his standards of perfection, then he will become indignant. He will spread his arms at the sides, with the palms up, in that characteristic stance of perfectionist incredulity. "How could you let that happen? Didn't you realize that...? What is going on here?" If criticized, he will respond immediately and arrogantly in defense, with no prior reflection on the merits of the criticism, like a porcupine bristling its quills. If angered, he becomes sarcastic and ill-mannered; he becomes rude and he shouts. He may become involved in shouting matches, or even fisticuffs, in public with strangers. And if his pride or vanity is trampled upon, he may be incited to the narcissistic-perfectionistic-aggressive blind NPA super-rage, which has been described earlier. The intensity of this red-faced rage may shock others seeing it for the first time. Many NPA individuals are intensely aware of this tendency and consciously attempt to keep a tight lid on their emotions, so that in fact the rage appears only infrequently.

If an NPA individual is subjugated in a long-term relationship with a companion or mate, and in particular by a "power behind the throne", then for much of his daily life his aggressive component will be strongly muted. He may thus appear as an individual somewhat placidly riding the merry-go-round of life, apparently little motivated and somehow "lacking in ambition".

Moving on to an NPA individual who is overtly power-seeking, he is sometimes grandiloquent, and he may lose all sense of propriety. One senses that he is often making a conscious effort to be not overly overbearing or too dominating. He assumes leadership because he thinks — nay he knows — that he is the best one for the job. But despite his efforts to convince others and himself that he is not aggressive in a cutthroat manner, he has a pervasive inward feeling that no one should push him around and that he should attain heights of excellence — that he should succeed to the very limits of his ambition. As in other aggressive types, but in a form muted by his sense of duty, there emerges the deep conviction that he should be above the masses and above the competition. It is a conviction fed by narcissistic ambition acting synergistically with his innate aggressive drive, with both being forged and tempered by the behavioral complex of perfectionism.

If he aspires to be "the boss", then the boss he is — there is no question about it — and his sense of restraint may fade. He may reveal a barely camouflaged arrogance. He then requires that his instinct for perfectionism be fulfilled. He requires that others pay constant attention to the details that his sense of "doing things well" requires. He demands "spit and polish". He insists on punctuality. He requires the continual approbation of his colleagues but would be embarrassed by their overt adulation.

He will dominate the conversation in a group. He tends to speak compulsively at conferences. If a difference of opinion arises, he will become agitated and will feel that he must have the last word.

He has pride in his honesty. Overt prevarication is anathema to him. However, to maintain his position of dominance, which he somehow feels in his bones is a right granted to him directly from the heavens, he will have no compunction with regard to the withholding of information that his opponents might use against him.

If he is not so much a boss than an upcoming achiever, for example in a hierarchal structure, then he becomes an "expert" in some field. Once his area of expertise is established it tends to expand in two ways. First, it expands in his own mind so that he becomes an expert not just in his narrow field but in the broader areas of technology, science, education or philosophy. Second, it becomes, by his own word of mouth, disseminated in time and space: everyone should have the benefit of his expertise.

Despite his often overbearing demeanor he has pride in his manners, in decorum, and he rarely would insult an individual to his face. Vindictiveness toward others and sadistic behavior may be overt, it is true, but usually it is well camouflaged and only subtly present. It may take the form of apparently good-natured but persistent teasing of a subordinate or opponent, being condescending toward him, overpowering him in public under a mass of sarcastic verbiage, or in that passive vindictive triumph that has been classic since time immemorial, simply leaving without saying good-bye.

As a leader or as a head of the family, he becomes an autocrat and cannot tolerate insubordination. He is the classic martinet with panache. The slightest indication of disloyalty may be dealt with unbounded harshness, and no punishment, even corporal punishment, will be excessive. Family members will not be exempt. Although others may stand aghast at the intensity of his vengeance, to his own mind he is a misunderstood man of mercy whose hand is occasionally forced to mete out harsh justice. In such circumstances his only saving grace is that he tends to mellow with age.

As an aggressive type, the NPA individual certainly "plays the game" of dominance and submission, but the "game" is often muted by his sense of duty. His aggressive tendencies are moderated by the behavioral complex of perfectionism, but in the framework of narcissistic behavior, the resultant character structure is very different from that of the PA type. In marriage he will usually be a devoted and faithful to his mate. But if the relationship goes awry, he will become a somewhat passive "situational sadist" and may finally attempt to extricate himself. He may be sexually promiscuous. In other words, his sense of duty has limits.

Finally, like his cousin the NP type, he too has made a "deal with life", though in muted form. If he takes care of the business of life, then the business of life should take care of him. And if it does not, then life's failures are taken very, very hard, subjecting this active, vigorous individual to the depths of an abject state. When he falls, it is all the more painful, because it is, in his own mind, the mighty who has fallen.

In the final analysis, this individual, too, is a prisoner of his character structure, and he is puzzled by the demons that seem to be driving him in three different directions. His life may be one of constant turbulence as he tries to streamline his narcissistic, perfectionistic and aggressive traits into a cohesive unity, all the while trying to keep a lid on his NPA super-rage. And it is only in looking into his character structure that he may begin to create for himself a life situation that is compatible with psychic survival in his human society.

4

Inhibited Aggression:
Passive Aggressive types

We now describe a second category of NPA types in which the trait of aggression is genetically inhibited from an early age: the *Passive Aggressive* types.

(In the next chapter, we present another category of inhibited aggressive types, the Resigned types, in which the trait of aggression is constrained by environmental factors after maturity).

In Passive Aggressive types, trait A is genetically partially inhibited "congenitally", or from birth. We append one minus sign (–) or two minus signs (=) to the letter A, according to whether trait A is only partially or profoundly inhibited. We call the A– types *non-compliant* types and the A= types *compliant* types.

We obtain the following Passive Aggressive types:

NPA– NPA= sanguine perfectionistic
NA– NA= sanguine non- perfectionistic

These types are *sanguine types,* meaning that they have the N trait [8].

Inhibition of trait A

Inhibited aggression in the Passive Aggressive types may be best described as the trait of "deference" or "non-confrontation." Although social relationships can be varied and complex, especially when they become stressful, Passive Aggressive types tend to gravitate toward avoidance of conflict and to relative submissiveness in social relations.

We noted in the previous chapter that *Dominant types* having the A trait can be reduced to a temporary subdued A– state of relative submission during social interactions, typically when an individual enters into a relationship with a stronger companion. In contrast, in *Passive Aggressive types* the A– or A= state is determined from birth by genes and is a stable, baseline state of relative submissiveness that can be identified in a child at an early age.

Because of the lability of the A trait, non-compliant Passive Aggressive types can mimic the A+ state of Dominant types, albeit usually for short periods of time. In this state, the behavior of NA– and NPA– individuals can superficially resemble that of the NA and NPA Dominant types, respectively.

Behaviorisms associated with Passive Aggressive types during routine social interactions are similar to those that occur in Dominant types under conditions of stress. These are in the realm of generally restrained behavior, tentative gestures, nervousness and a voice with speech hesitation or tremor.

The P trait in Passive Aggressive types

As in the case of Dominant types, in Passive Aggressive types the presence of the P trait can have a profound influence on the expression of the N trait. In the *non-perfectionistic* NA– and NA= types, the N trait may appear in its "unbridled" form as narcissistic flamboyance in dress, gestures and behavior, in a greater tendency to exhibit the gingival smile, and in a higher degree of extroversion. In the *perfectionistic* NPA– and NPA= types, the expression of the N trait is usually well camouflaged because of the modulating effect of the P trait and an accompanying lower degree of extroversion.

[*Wikipedia & DonkeyHotey*]

Fig. 2. Caricatures of perfectionistic Passive Aggressive types. *Left:* compliant NPA= type. *Right:* non-compliant NPA− type.

Profiles

Below are brief summaries of the most common Passive Aggressive types. We present first the *perfectionistic* types (compliant NPA= and non-compliant NPA−), and then the *non-perfectionistic* types (compliant NA= and non-compliant NA−):

NPA= type

"Perfectionistic compliant type"

In *compliant* types, the trait A is profoundly suppressed, so that whatever the circumstances they tend not exhibit aggressive behavior in competitive social situations. They can exhibit the aggressive "A rage", but this is rare. Compliant types tend to be introverted and may seek a life style involving little responsibility and much protection. Sexually promiscuous individuals are vulnerable to abusive relationships and may have a tendency to masochistic behavior.

Rage: "N rage", "A rage" or combined "NA rage". In most compliant individuals the rages are rarely seen.

Also known as: "Perfectionistic compliant submissive type". "NP like" compliant type. "The Quiet Achiever". Depressive, masochistic personality. Submissive, dependent or self-effacing personality. "The shrinking violet".

Complexion: Tending toward sanguine or flushed in individuals of light skin color. Blushes very easily with embarrassment.

Smile: Warm smile when at ease. Otherwise nervous smile.

Photograph: Uncomfortable before camera in unfamiliar settings.

Voice: Nervous voice pattern with speech hesitation or tremor. Low in intensity.

Gestures: Reserved and tentative.

Handwriting: Neat and legible, as a slave writing for his masters.

Sexuality: Tendency to promiscuity: low. Tendency to LGBT in sexual orientation: moderate.

Color preference: Conservative in color choice.

Population genetics: "The Introspective Habitancy". See Passive Aggressive NPA− type.

Susceptibilities: Shyness. Masochism. Sadomasochistic "morbid dependency" as the dependent partner. Social phobia. Panic disorder. Reactive depression. Dependent, avoidant personality disorder. See also Passive Aggressive NPA− type.

Pitfalls: NPA= individuals can superficially resemble NP, NPA− or Borderline types.

Character caricature [9]

This introverted individual carries the mottos, "I am the most unselfish, the most sympathetic and the most loving," or "I will do anything, but anything for you so long as you protect me for the rest of my life."

He has, perhaps without realizing it, lacked aggressive tendencies from early childhood. He may be a self-conscious, painfully shy "shrinking violet" and be easy prey to any aggressive type. He may have a strong feeling, or a vague uncomfortable suspicion, that all was not well during his very early childhood. Somehow, he feels and acts as if, in the deep recesses of his mind, he were ashamed of something that he is, guilty of something that he did wrong or something he should have done right, or was somehow, somewhere deeply humiliated before others.

Being defenseless, and easily frightened, he fears any demands to be made upon him, particularly those forcing him to any position of responsibility. In fact, the words "responsibility", "ambition", "career" or "success" are taboo to him, and may send shivers down his spine. If he finds himself in a hierarchal structure, he wants to stay right where he is. He certainly does not want to move up to a position of greater responsibility, and he will invoke the "Peter Principle" in his defense. That is, he will say that he does not want to exceed the limits of his capabilities, which despite intensive rationalization, must have become painfully obvious to him.

Although his aggressive qualities have been suppressed into profound submission, they are nevertheless latently present. He does "play the game" of dominance and submission, but instinctively feels himself helpless at the bottom of the "pecking order". In his helplessness, his only salvation in life is to offer to all comers helpfulness, love, sympathy, compassion and self-sacrifice.

In love relationships the "shrinking violet" flourishes into a "clinging vine", and he "falls in love" in the form of a morbid dependency with almost any strong individual. And if he obtains a commitment for protection, it must be total. He must have everything done for him, while in return he offers little else than the promise of his total abandon to "true love".

In his insatiable desire to achieve safety in the promises of protection and love, he becomes vulnerable to abuse by others, and in fact, does come to feel that he is abused. He, thus, finds himself in the position of offering himself to be abused in order to fulfill the needs of his character structure and to find satisfaction in his life. Hence, it is in this character structure that we find the roots of *masochism*, that is, the finding of satisfaction in life through being abused by others. He may, in fact, be overtly sexually masochistic.

As with all of the character types, frustration of the most serious kind is engendered when the premises of the underlying character structure are threatened. For this individual, the worst threat is that of the loss of his protective master, boss or subjugator. This will be defended vigorously in the form of a claim of fidelity from the master. Since he, the slave, has been so faithful and loving, the master must respond in turn. The dynamics of such a "morbid dependency" are discussed in more detail elsewhere [9].

If frustration mounts to a breaking point, the individual may, finally, incite himself to an aggressive-vindictive rage. This will surely surprise his onlookers, who are used to seeing a very quiet, shy individual. It will also surprise and frighten the individual himself, who may not have known that a spirit of aggression lurked deep in the catacombs of his character.

If the hopelessness of the situation comes to the fore, then a deep abject state of depression will ensue. In this individual, the abject state is characterized by suffering, and the suffering provides a source of "positive feedback" to the unconscious motivations behind his basic character structure. That is, the suffering becomes a further reinforcing alibi for the individual's not mobilizing himself, and for his continuing demand that he be rescued by the master, or by anyone else, without any positive effort at all on his part.

The above descriptions would apply to introspective individuals of the NPA= and NA= types, who would superficially somewhat resemble the NP and N types, respectively. That is, the NPA= type would tend to be a quiet, meticulous perfectionist worker, while the NA= type would tend to be more labile, more aware of his physical and sexual attributes, and less a perfectionist worker than a task-oriented "doer"...

This individual's character structure, whatever its resultant complexity and whatever his real accomplishments in life, seems to be constructed around a nidus of a feeling of shame. He is an introvert. He has the so-called "inferiority complex".

He may be blandly passive or a true "shrinking violet". He has a low, restrained voice, and he is not articulate. His countenance suggests a trace of sadness. His movements are tentative and his gestures reserved. His eye contact with others is poor, as he displays the averted eyes of a slave before his masters, which in his case includes almost everyone with whom he comes in contact. He shrinks in the presence of kings, but also in the presence of shopkeepers.

Meeting people in a business or social situation is an ordeal for him. He forgets names as soon as the introductions are uttered. If he is required to make the introductions himself, his mind goes blank and he may enter a state of panic. He is very uncomfortable before a group of strangers. He lives in fear of being called upon to speak extemporaneously. If he must give a speech he will write it out word for word or commit it to memory, fearing that his mind will go blank when it comes time to deliver it. When he does deliver it, his nervousness is apparent, all the more so if his audience is hostile or in the least bit threatening. For the same reason this individual will not be seen on television unless he is accompanied by his master.

He will be uncomfortable and feel anxious if he must go to a social function where strangers will be present. What he fears most is a medium-sized group of six to twelve persons, where he might suddenly become the center of attention. Paradoxically, though, he yearns for the presence of others, and to stay home in loneliness is a state of shame that he tries to avoid or hide at all costs.

He has a poor self-image but does not try to bolster it. Even though he may possess the N trait of narcissism, he tends not to adorn himself excessively (but the NA= type may, indeed, adorn himself flamboyantly). His dress is usually reserved and may be outright shabby. In fact, any state of ostentatiousness is alien to him. If he sees himself suddenly in a mirror he may startle himself, and he is not particularly enamored by what he sees. He may at times consciously wish that he were not he, but someone else.

Having renounced competitiveness, he has all of his pride invested in helping others and in trying to please them. He is in his self-effacing way overhelpful, overkind, overcaring and oversympathetic. His handwriting, written as it is for the benefit of others, is nicely legible. And in his pride he sees himself, not as a selfish person whose claim is to be cared for throughout his journey through life, but as a selfless saint who is indispensable to his boss or to his mate and family.

His taboo on competitiveness and on any aspirations for himself pervades his entire life, from his important decisions of how to gain his livelihood and whom to marry, to the less important ones regarding the minutiae of his daily existence. Feeling as he does as a stowaway on the ship of life, he fears that if he does anything implying independence from his protectors then he might suddenly find himself in a lifeboat, alone at sea and having to fend for himself in the struggle for survival in his hostile world.

In space and time, he is something of a lost soul. He may have a magic circle, of ten-mile radius, from which he dare not leave. He may have only the vaguest idea of the locations of nearby states, cities or townships. He may not have the slightest idea where the maze of highways near his home actually leads. If he goes on a trip, he enjoys himself as he is piloted about by his protector, but he will have only the slightest idea in geographical terms where he has been. He is totally incapable of reading maps or transportation schedules, and may ascribe this inability to some kind of learning disability. In fact, if he is not taken somewhere, he would not dream of going alone. Hence, in contrast with the Resigned type whose pride is vested in complete independence, the compliant type has all of his pride invested in complete dependence on his protector, protectors or subjugator.

NPA− type

"Perfectionistic non-compliant type"

In *non-compliant* types, the trait A is partially suppressed, but depending on circumstances they can exhibit aggressive behavior in competitive social situations. Low-temperament individuals tend to be introverted, and the P trait of compulsive perfectionism is most noticed in those individuals. Higher temperament individuals can be "nervous extroverts", often with speech hesitancy or tremor.

Rage: "N rage", "A rage" or combined "NA rage". In most non-compliant individuals the A rage is uncommon.

Also known as: "Perfectionistic non-compliant submissive type". "NP like" non-compliant type. "The Agitated Achiever". The passive-aggressive personality. Reactive depressive personality. "Type A" personality of the medical literature.

Complexion: Tending toward sanguine or flushed in individuals of light skin color. Blushes easily with embarrassment.

Smile: Relaxed social smile rarely seen. Nervous smile.

Photograph: Usually uncomfortable before camera, sometimes to the extent of phobia. Mugs for camera.

Voice: Nervous voice pattern with speech hesitation. Silent when under stress.

Gestures: Agitated, inconsistent and tentative.

Handwriting: Usually legible but "jerky" quality, with large variations in size of letters. Sometimes slurred. Sometimes messy corrections.

Sexuality: Tendency to promiscuity: moderate. Tendency to LGBT in sexual orientation: moderately high.

Color preference: Variable according to the individual and situation, but usually there is a discomfort with bright or ostentatious colors.

Population genetics: "The Introspective Habitancy", having a high prevalence of NPA− types, and moderate prevalence of NP and NPA types. Example: Anglo-Saxon subpopulations, Finland.

Susceptibilities: Shyness. Social phobia. Public speaking phobia. Speech hesitation, tremor, stuttering. Avoidant personality disorder. Panic disorder. Reactive depression. Narcissistic personality disorder (NPD, in dominant role). Sadomasochistic "morbid dependency" as either the dominant or dependent partner. Coronary artery disease ("Type A" personality).

Pitfalls: Unstressed NPA− individuals can resemble NP types. High temperament NP types can resemble NPA− types. Socially active Passive Aggressive types can have behavior that could be confused with that of N or NA types. Introverted Borderline types can resemble Passive Aggressive types.

Character caricature [9]

The character structure of the non-compliant type is similar to that of the compliant type. That is, this individual is not a forceful person and may even be a shy, self-conscious introvert. We noted that the compliant type views his life from the bottom of the "pecking order" and is quite satisfied to stay there, somewhat contentedly awaiting retirement and death, provided that he is well taken care of and protected. However, whereas the non-compliant type also views life from the bottom of the pecking order, he has one eye open toward the top and aspires to achieve power, glory and domination, even if ever so briefly.

He does, in fact, retain his narcissistic behavioral trait, even though his aggressive capacities have been stunted (NPA− and NA− types). He is, therefore, in the constant throes of an intrapsychic conflict. He desires narcissistic glory, but he lacks the aggressive power to support his ambitious drive. In competitive society he may be so unsure of himself, and fraught with stage-fright, that at the same time that he craves the limelight, he also fears it. In overtly stressful circumstances, he begins to glance about in search of protection or escape, like the classic coward who dies a thousand deaths.

He can ascend to an energetic A+ state for only a brief period, and he is quite apprehensive and vulnerable there if he is in competitive surroundings. If he encounters an aggressive type in competition with him while in the energetic state, he becomes agitated, uncomfortable, easily intimidated, and is usually easily defeated. He may find himself behaving like a frightened rabbit. For one so low to have aspired so high, the agony of defeat is severely stressful. Not only does he come crashing down to his original A− state of submissiveness in an abrupt personality split, but he may also enter an abject state of depression because of his failure. With repeated failures, he may become more and more wary of any aggressive ventures, or even of assertive behavior toward others of lower status. He may develop phobias or "panic attacks" with respect to situations in which he has previously felt himself to be humiliated.

Finally, he comes to temper somewhat his desires for glory. He will convince himself that somehow, in this life anyway, he was not meant to accomplish those glorious deeds of his visions. He becomes an opportunist and a dreamer. If opportunity knocks and presents itself to him, with little danger of his being overcome or humiliated in the presence of aggressive types, then he will abruptly split his personality to the energetic state and seize the opportunity by the horns. If he is lucky, he will descend to his baseline submissive state of his own accord, with the victory intact. To this individual "nature abhors a vacuum", and if a vacuum presents itself he will step into the situation. If thrown into a lifeboat with stronger types, he will be quite content to stay submissive. But if the others are weaker, then he will take command, and command he will. In the land of the blind, the one-eyed man is king!

The love relationships of this character type are, as one may have guessed, often based on the "morbid dependency", and he may adopt the role of subjugator or subjugated, or even both simultaneously in a love triangle. Using the most blunt of terminology of psychiatry, he may assume the role of either a hardened sadistic master, or of a suffering masochistic lover desirous of nothing in life except to lose himself completely in a warm, tender, sentimental love of subjugation to another individual.

As with any individual possessing the trait of aggression, if the individual adopts the dominant role in a relationship of subjugation, or to the extent that he comes to consider himself above any person or group of people, then aggressive-sadistic trends may come to the fore. These may show themselves in several ways:

First, the aggressive sadistic behavior may be overt, especially if the individual is incited to one of his rare aggressive-vindictive rages. If goaded into a barroom fight, this type can become a wild panther, and he may not stop until no one is left standing and until every bottle in the barroom is broken.

Second, if the circumstances present themselves, he may become paranoid and quietly manipulative, hence similar in behavior to a PA type.

Third, he may become a "situational sadist" if he is tied to a relationship with a companion or mate from which, because of life circumstances, he cannot extricate himself.

Finally, his ventures to the energetic state of aggression if frequent and short-lived, may become transient states of exhilaration, or thrills.

As may be predicted, NA− and NPA− individuals would have behavioral characteristics somewhat similar to N and NP Dominant individuals, respectively. In addition to being incitable to aggressive-vindictive rages, the NA− and NPA− types would also be capable of narcissistic or combined NA rages.

What finally emerges in the non-compliant Passive Aggressive character type is a basically introverted, active, even hyperactive, individual who may be capable of assuming practically any psychic state of any of the other character types. He may be meekly submissive or even masochistic. He can be sadistic. He can go into the wildest of rages and be depressed into the deepest of abject states. He can split his personality to aggressive behavior, and back to the submissive state in a flash. He can see the "morbid dependency" from both ends, even simultaneously. He may go into flurries of introspective narcissistic-perfectionist work activity of the NP type, or of hypersexual activity of the NA+ type. He may feel like an NPA+ king, or he may be drawn by circumstances to the psychopathic aggression of a PA+ individual. He seems to have the widest range of psychic states and the widest range possible of emotions. He has ability to empathize with practically any of the other character types but not necessarily to sympathize with them. That is, he may be to feel what his subjugated partner is feeling, but not necessarily able to offer his love and sympathy to him…

This individual appears to be an introvert who periodically seems to come out of his shell. His demeanor, in fact, is highly dependent on the circumstances of the moment.

His baseline personality is essentially that of an affable compliant type, and his facial features often show that characteristic trace of sadness. But his car is parked outside, with the engine running, and it may be a sport model capable of flying him to the pinnacles of the glory of his imagination. Thus, this individual has a subtle, or sometimes not so subtle, agitated, fidgeting demeanor, as if he wants to go somewhere. He fidgets with his hair, his hands, his moustache, as if they were masturbatory equivalents suggesting repressed sexual yearnings. In stressful situations his eye contact with others is abysmal, and indeed he often has the wandering eyes of perpetual apprehension. His handwriting often reflects his agitation, and it is often barely legible, with many corrections, or else well-formed but jerky.

He is a compliant type who appears to be highly motivated, and indeed that he is. But more often than not his objectives in life are unclear. He would like desperately to succeed in life, but his ambition lacks the necessary aggressive component, and he would avoid using the word "career". He seems to scrutinize a ship as it passes, and he jumps on it in the hope that it will take him to reasonable success. But he, too, deep in his heart, feels that he is a stowaway on board.

The dynamics of this individual were presented earlier and will not be repeated here in detail. To summarize, he is an opportunist, a dreamer. He is introspective, sometimes a shy individual who requires privacy. He has something of a free spirit, and may be a traveler. He periodically aspires to heights and crashes to depths, like a majestic eagle whose wings have been clipped. He knows the thrills and exhilarations of the conquests of his Dominant cousins, but he knows that his successes in the realm of aggressive behavior are of the hit-and-run variety, and that he cannot have aspiration to domination or to effective leadership in a career.

If he does ascend to a position of leadership on the basis of his affability or his intellectual qualities, he does not inspire confidence before his colleagues and subordinates. He is frequently very self-conscious. If at all intimidated, he becomes tongue-tied; his voice loses its forcefulness, and he tends to fidget and to stammer or mumble. Even if he is an expert in his field he cannot mount the podium with any confidence to speak extemporaneously. He exasperates others with his indecisiveness, as he tries to please everyone. He is vulnerable to the views of any strong personality, and as he is at the mercy of the last person with whom he speaks, he may be constantly changing his views. Thus, others will accuse him of being "good-natured" but "weak minded". Often they will misinterpret his apprehensive reticence for cynical indifference. His basic attitude toward life is seen in his usual photograph: he is not comfortable looking at the camera, and often he is not smiling.

In love relations he may assume any role in the "game", and he may lead a rather quiet life, playing either the dominant or submissive role of subjugation. If he is not too shy and is successful in competitive society, he is exceedingly vulnerable to being subjugated by a "power behind the throne". Alternatively, he too may assume the role of a quiet hunter or "bird of prey". In fact, he and the NA type are often both out on the prowl, looking for each other, and when they meet sparks are bound to fly. More often than not, an affair of the "lightning and thunder" variety begins, and exciting and exhilarating as it may appear, it is usually destined to achieve no lasting stability. As has been described earlier, sadomasochistic elements inevitably seep into the relationship, the two partners never really gain an understanding of their own or each other's needs and motivations, and the relationship comes to an end when the NA partner moves on to a new companion to continue the chain reaction.

Finally, we see the frustration that the non-compliant type faces throughout his active life. He has a strong sense of narcissistic ambition but a stunted component of aggression. And during his jerky ride through life he finds that others do not particularly admire his jerkiness, are ill at ease with him, and he often finds himself isolated. Sometimes he, too, seems to be a speedboat out of control in a fogbound harbor, and it is only in looking at his own basic character structure that he can begin to lift the fog and bring himself under control.

NA− and NA= types

Non-perfectionistic types:

- **Non-compliant type, NA−**
- **Compliant type, NA=**

In *non-compliant* types, the trait A is partially suppressed, but depending on circumstances they can exhibit aggressive behavior in competitive social situations. In *compliant* types, the trait A is profoundly suppressed, so that whatever the circumstances they tend not exhibit aggressive behavior in competitive social situations.

The NA− and NA= types distinguish themselves from their close cousins, the NPA− and NPA= types, in lacking the P trait of perfectionism. The A trait is partially suppressed, but depending on the circumstances NA− individuals can exhibit aggressive behavior in competitive social situations. Since the P trait is lacking in the NA− and NA= types, the sanguine N trait may be overtly and flamboyantly expressed as "unbridled narcissism", as if these individuals were introverted, submissive or nervous N or NA types.

[Wikipedia]

Fig. 3. Caricature of a non-perfectionistic Passive Aggressive NA− type.

Rage: "N rage", "A rage" or combined "NA rage".

Also known as: "N like" Passive Aggressive types.

Complexion: Tending toward sanguine or flushed in individuals of light skin color. Blush very easily.

Smile: Warm smile when at ease. Otherwise nervous smile.

Photograph: Uncomfortable before camera in unfamiliar settings. Mugs for camera.

Voice: Nervous voice pattern with speech hesitation.

Gestures: More expressive than in perfectionistic Passive Aggressive types.

Handwriting: Non-perfectionistic.

Sexuality: Tendency to promiscuity and to LGBT in sexual orientation: high (higher than in the perfectionistic Passive Aggressive types).

Color preference: Preference for bright and multicolors, akin to the Dominant non-perfectionistic N and NA types.

Population genetics: Similar to the perfectionistic Passive Aggressive types, NPA= and NPA−.

Susceptibilities: Similar to the perfectionistic Passive Aggressive types. Bipolar, Borderline personality disorder. Attention deficit disorders: ADD/ADHD. Asperger syndrome. Shyness. Public speaking phobia. Social phobia. Speech hesitation, tremor, stuttering. Panic disorder. Eating disorders. Reactive depression. Narcissistic personality disorder (NPD, in dominant role). Sadomasochistic "morbid dependency" as either the dominant or dependent partner.

Pitfalls: Depending on temperament and other factors, NA= and NA− individuals can superficially resemble the N or NA Dominant types, the NPA= and NPA− Passive Aggressive types, or Borderline types.

Character caricature [9]

We now turn to the NA− type, keeping in mind the three basic attributes that rule his life: unbridled narcissism, non-perfectionism, and submission. In fact, the two traits of unbridled narcissism and submission seem to be continually acting in antagonism in this personage, so that sometimes he appears as an affable extrovert, and sometimes as a submissive introvert. In addition, lack of the behavioral complex of perfectionism often gives his character structure a labile, fragile quality.

Once the character structure of this personage is recognized, one can predict his general behavior, almost as if it were a foregone conclusion. In real life he appears as an affable, sanguine-complexioned, somewhat subdued individual who, despite his generally submissive nature, is ever ready to respond to the call of the limelight. If his life situation supports him so that his unbridled narcissism comes to the fore, then he may be somewhat expansive or even charismatic. He tends to adorn himself or "dress up" — sometimes strikingly — to a much greater extent than his NPA− cousin, and indeed this is often the most obvious superficial difference between these two types. He may, in short, display any of the attributes that we have come to associate with the charming, but often flighty, N character type.

If he trends toward being a compliant submissive type, he is exactly that − however much he would like to ignore or deny this facet of his personality. His tendency to be sympathetic and agreeable pervades his daily life, and his acquaintances will invariably consider him to be a "nice person". However, having a remnant of the trait of aggression, he reveals himself to be a "player of the game" of dominance and submission in stressful situations, being susceptible not only to red-faced narcissistic rages but also — albeit rarely — to the aggressive-vindictive rage.

In competitive society his submissive trait sooner or later becomes evident. When challenged, he is easily intimidated, and others will say that "he can't seem to get it all together", or will accuse him of "bumbling" or of "histrionics". If he comes to power on the basis of his narcissistic charisma, at the highest level of society, then he requires much support from his entourage in his attempts to achieve his grandiose visions of unbridled glory. Hence, he is easily subjugated, and indeed, hovering in the wings there is often seen a protective, perfectionist "power behind the throne", always ready to ensure that everything will progress with the precision of a well-oiled machine.

In adolescence, the NA− type is an active but reserved individual who will often describe himself as being "on the shy side". Nevertheless, his unbridled narcissism is continually seeking to overcome his submissive shyness, and he may be attracted to expansive, soaring projects, again reminiscent of the activities of the self-flaunting N character type. He may, in fact, be attracted to public speaking, to a career in modeling, to the stage, or to the dance.

If he aspires to be an actor, he may be highly successful in his portrayal of the affable, kind-hearted − but perennially abused hero or heroine. Often, however, he is only moderately successful, since his generally submissive nature continually intrudes into his desire to be the forceful personality of his dreams...

Like his cousin the NPA− type, the NA− personage may lead a successful, relatively calm existence if his life situation is well supportive. If it is not, then this labile personality is prone to transient masochistic love affairs, hypochondria, phobias, fugues, panic attacks, agitated reactive depressions, as well as episodes of euphoria and hysteria.

5

Inhibited Aggression: Resigned types

In the prior chapter we presented a category of inhibited aggression in which the A trait of aggression was genetically inhibited from birth: the Passive Aggressive types. In this chapter, we present another category, the *Resigned* types, in which the trait of aggression is partially suppressed very differently, by environmental factors.

Resigned types

Resigned types are those individuals in whom the trait of aggression is inhibited by constraining environmental factors after maturity (notation −A).

We obtain the following Resigned types:

NP−A sanguine perfectionistic
N−A sanguine non-perfectionistic

These types are both sanguine types, meaning that they have the N trait [*10*].

Inhibition of trait A in Resigned types

Individuals of the Resigned type are mature individuals who previously interacted socially on the basis of the trait of aggression in the context of relationships of dominance and submission.

We identify two groups of Resigned types, namely:

1. former Dominant types (NA or NPA), and

2. former non-compliant Passive Aggressive types (NA− or NPA−).

Whereas inhibited aggression in the Passive Aggressive types was described as the trait of "deference" or "non-confrontation", in Resigned types it is more in the realm of "avoidance" or "detachment". Because of environmental factors, or "stress", the individual becomes detached, or abdicates from competitive social interaction in order to devote himself to a more serene, independent life style.

We noted earlier that Dominant types having the A trait and non-compliant Passive Aggressive types can vary their status of aggression between A+ and A− states of relative dominance and submission during social interactions. In contrast, the Resigned types, having chosen a life style of independence, actively choose to avoid such interactions as a way of life.

The P trait in Resigned types

As in the case of the Dominant and Passive Aggressive types, the P trait can have a profound tempering influence on the expression of the N trait. In particular, in the non-perfectionistic N−A type, despite an underlying life style of detachment, the N trait may appear in its unbridled form as unrestrained "narcissism" in dress, in social and sexual behavior, in a greater tendency to exhibit the gingival smile, and generally in a higher degree of extroversion.

Profiles

Below are brief summaries of the two most common Resigned types. We present first the *perfectionistic* type (NP −A), and then the *non-perfectionistic* type (N −A):

NP −A and N −A types

- **Perfectionistic type, NP −A**
- **Non-perfectionistic type, N −A**

Behavior associated with Resigned types will depend on the individual's NPA type before detachment (*Dominant* or *Passive Aggressive*; *perfectionistic* or *non-perfectionistic*). If the individual succeeds in his or her goal of non-stressful independence, behaviorisms associated with the A trait will be muted. In such circumstances, the NP −A and N−A Resigned types may strongly resemble the non-aggressive Dominant types NP and N, respectively.

Rage: "N rage", "A rage" or combined "NA rage". In Resigned types the rages are rarely seen.

Also known as: Sanguine resigned. Avoidant or detached personality.

Complexion: Tending toward sanguine or flushed in individuals of light skin color, especially in former Passive Aggressive types.

Smile: Former NPA and NA types: smiles easily. Former Passive Aggressive types: relaxed social smile rarely seen.

Photograph: Former NPA and NA types: relaxed. Former Passive Aggressive types: camera-shy.

Voice: Depends on former NPA type.

Gestures: Reserved.

Handwriting: Usually neat and legible.

Sexuality: Variable according to life situation. Wary of strong attachments.

Color preference: Variable according to the individual and situation, but usually there is a discomfort with bright or ostentatious colors.

Population genetics: Etiology of Resigned types is highly dependent on environmental factors.

Susceptibilities: Former Dominant types: see NPA and NA types. Former Passive Aggressive types: see *compliant* and *non-compliant* types.

Pitfalls: Unless details of the individuals' lives are known, descriptions of the Resigned types NP−A and N−A can mimic NP and N types, respectively. Resigned types can resemble Borderline types.

Character caricature [11]

Resigned types are mature individuals having an aggressive component in their character structure, who have given up the struggle of "playing the game" of dominance and submission, and have entered a state of detachment. We denote the state of suppressed aggression after maturity by −A. We identify two groups of Resigned types: 1) former Dominant types having the trait of aggression, and 2) former non-compliant Passive Aggressive types. Such individuals carry the mottos: "I am self-sufficient. I am independent of everyone and everything," and "I don't need anyone else, thus no one can hurt me."

Whatever the cause for the detachment, whether it was rooted in genetics, in a single traumatic event such as a disfiguring accident, or in a spectrum of stressful circumstances, the individual has, in essence, taken to the hills. He has felt his psychic equilibrium to be in jeopardy, and in defense he has rationalized a philosophy of resourcefulness and splendid inner independence. He becomes an onlooker of life, or to the extent that he considers himself to be superior to others, he may adopt the attitude of a detached overseer.

NP −A type

Considering first the NP−A type, he develops a personal philosophy of non-involvement with all things both great and small, perhaps a philosophy of equilibrium or communication with nature. His philosophy may be based on achieving peace through religion or through non-involvement with the environment. As he would consider his involvement with the environment a desecration of the natural order, so does he resent any intrusion of the environment into his life. He will resist acceptance of any philosophy or any way of thinking that may lead to irresolvable problems or to unforeseen conflicts. He may deny the evidence of Darwinian evolution, thereby assuming ultimate independence from the world around him in effectively denying that he is a member of the human race.

He develops his own magic circle of detachment and bitterly resents any unwanted intrusion into it. There is an undercurrent of anxiety with regard to being intruded upon or of being drawn into circumstances that would impose themselves on him. He is constantly scanning the horizon for the approach of events casting their shadows before them, and he is always prepared for escape if the coercion becomes too great. If an escape route is not available, then his anxiety level will rise. He may be literally claustrophobic in constrained situations.

His whole life becomes geared to the maintenance of his detachment. He will seek work in a non-hierarchal structure where the fewest demands are made on him. He will, at all costs, avoid making demands on others. He may become a physician, a taxi driver, a free-lance writer, a nun, a lighthouse keeper or a vagabond. If coerced, he will leave his job abruptly, and the search for another suitable one may take an interminably long time. In sports he is an avid spectator, or if he is active he will row a single scull or be a cross-country jogger.

His personal life is often a mystery to his companions and co-workers. Often no one really knows where he lives or what he does. He may keep an unlisted telephone number and no identifying sign on his door. In a hotel, a "do not disturb" sign appears immediately on his door. He lives and travels alone. And to all observers he appears to live alone and like it.

He is, of course, unaggressive. He is friendly, cordial and good humored. He is reliable, helpful and has a real sense of integrity. He is a person who is well liked by others and is considered to be dependable.

In order to maintain his detachment he must continually be on guard so that friendships do not become overly constraining. Relationships with a sexual connotation become interludes with the understanding that real involvement is not around the corner. The prospect of marriage is frightening unless his prospective mate is able to show the promise of supporting his detached status. His aversion to close friendships and to the expression of giving oneself to another person cannot help but lead to an emotional numbness. He becomes bland and phlegmatic. As he goes through life and is exposed to more and more, he responds by taking less and less. His life has become peaceful, placid with not a conflict in sight, but it has become shallow.

When threatened or goaded, he can be activated to an aggressive state, but like the non-compliant Passive Aggressive type, he is not comfortable there. He will be deeply disappointed with himself that others were able to penetrate his aura of placidity and goad him into "playing the game" once more.

When coerced to the breaking point, he may, once in a lifetime, erupt in a vociferous rage of rebellion, which carries the motto, "To hell with you all! I am not going to do all these things for you anymore! I'm getting out of here!" which will be seen to be a narcissistic rage in disguise.

When not coerced, this NP–A type is a quiet, resourceful worker who has a strong resemblance to the NP Dominant type, "the quiet achiever". However, the Resigned type's residual aggressive component is subtly evident by his occasional aggressive language and gestures. Like all types expressing the aggressive gene, he is prone to the undercurrents of sadistic behavior. In the detached individual this may occur in the form of passive obstructionist behavior reminiscent of the PA type, in the form of non-involvement in situations where disaster is imminent, in the morbid interest in natural disasters such as the following of the progress of a hurricane, or finally in simply standing back in detached amusement and watching the faults and foibles of others as they fritter and flounder about, fumble and fail in their frenetic ventures of futile human folly.

N –A type

Turning to the N–A Resigned type, according to the model he is lacking in perfectionist qualities. He is less a quiet worker than a narcissistic individual who is well capable of task-oriented accomplishments, but less of directed efforts requiring the planning and execution of many interrelated details. In addition, when activated to the NA+ state, he may resemble the hyperactive, hypersexual "bird of prey" NA type. In such an individual, his only bridge to involvement with others is on a sexual plane, and of course the affairs can lead to no stable relationship.

Finally, as is true for all character types, the Resigned type is vulnerable. If his magic circle comes to be repeatedly penetrated, he may feel the walls of life closing in on him, and he may descend into the profound depression of an abject state...

The Resigned types NP−A and N−A are much like NPA and NA types in totally unstressed circumstances. The voice is often somewhat subdued, yet it is usually more forceful, and has greater range, than that of the NP type. The NP−A type preserves the intimate eye contact of his NPA+ cousin. With regard to countenance, the NP−A and N−A types tend toward a sanguine complexion, while the non-sanguine −A and P−A types (schizoid Borderline individuals) tend toward pallor.

The Resigned type often reveals himself not so much by his mannerisms, the tone of his voice or his smile as by the detached life that he leads. In his serenity and in his non-involvement in close relationships he puzzles his colleagues and acquaintances, who may suspect that he has an unconventional sexual orientation. The dynamics of his lifestyle become understandable once his underlying character structure is apparent.

Somerset Maugham was obviously fascinated by resigned persons. The protagonist, Larry, of his biographical novel *The Razor's Edge* is a resigned vagabond, and individuals of the Resigned type appear in other of his works as well [12].

6

Inheritance of the NPA Traits

It is not necessary for one to know the genetic mechanisms underlying the NPA model to understand the model and apply it to one's daily life. However, to evaluate a family pedigree of any complexity, one will need to understand a few basic concepts of genetics. In particular, you will need to appreciate the definitions of *phenotype* and *genotype*, and the difference between *dominance* and *recessiveness*. A review of some of these concepts is included in the Glossary and in Appendix A.

Dominant types

On the basis of typical family pedigrees, we posited that the NPA traits are inherited according to the mechanisms of classical genetics [*13*]. In particular, the three traits:

1) obey the rule of independent assortment, and

2) follow an autosomal mechanism of transmission, with traits N and A being recessive, and P being dominant.

In simple terms, this means that the NPA traits obey the traditional laws of Mendelian genetics, with the genes underlying the traits being neither chromosomally linked together, nor sex-linked.

The possible combinations of genes (genotypes) consistent with the various NPA types (phenotypes) are shown below in Table 1. The phenotypes listed are the Dominant types of the model, corresponding to full expression of the three NPA traits.

The recessive alleles of the N and A traits are denoted by **n** and **a,** while the dominant allele of the P trait is denoted by the capital letter **P**.

Table 1

Genotypes of the Dominant NPA types

Phenotype	*Genotype*
N	(nn) (nna)
A	(aa) (naa)
NA	(nnaa)
NP	(nnP) (nnPP) (nnPa) (nnPPa)
PA	(Paa) (PPaa) (nPaa) (nPPaa)
NPA	(nnPaa) (nnPPaa)

Table 1 shows that an individual of a particular NPA type could have one of several possible genotypes. For example, the N type has two possibilities for its underlying genotype, namely **(nn)** and **(nna)**, depending on whether or not the individual is a silent carrier of the recessive **a** allele. In contrast, the NP type has four possibilities, depending, in addition, whether the dominant **P** allele is present in the homozygous or heterozygous state.

Note that the NA type has only one possible genotype, the fully homozygous state **(nnaa)**.

Possible offspring of Dominant NPA types

For convenience, we have tabulated the possible NPA types of the offspring according to the NPA types of the parents. Allowing for all possible genotypes in the parents, we present in Table 2 the possible NPA types in the children. To read the table, one locates the NPA types of the father and mother on the horizontal and vertical axes, with the area of intersection displaying the possible NPA types in the offspring. For example, one can see that in a parental mating of NA×NP, the children could be only of the four types: N, NP, NA or NPA.

	N	A	NP	NA	PA	NPA
N	N NA	"	"	"	"	"
A	N NA A	NA A	"	"	"	"
NP	N NP NA NPA	N NP NA NPA PA A	N NP NA NPA	"	"	"
NA	N NA	NA A	N NP NA NPA	NA	"	"
PA	N NP NA NPA PA A	NA NPA PA A	N NP NA NPA PA A	NA NPA PA A	NA NPA PA A	"
NPA	N NP NA NPA	NA NPA PA A	N NP NA NPA	NA NPA	NA NPA PA A	NA NPA
FATHER OR MOTHER	N	A	NP	NA	PA	NPA

Table 2. Dominant types: Possible NPA types in offspring according to the types of the father and mother (on either axis).

One can see from Table 2 that the restrictions on the possible NPA types of the offspring vary markedly according to the types of the parents.

Non-viable types and infertility

In addition to the six possible NPA types in the offspring shown in Table 2, the model generates two other phenotypes that are unlike any of the parental types. These are the P and 0 (null) "non-viable types", as shown in Table 3 below. We recognize these types as being "non-viable" because they lack expression of either the N or A trait.

Table 3
Non-viable types in progeny

Phenotype	*Genotype*
P	(nPa) (nPPa)
0 (null)	(na)

Therefore, the model quite unexpectedly predicts *infertility* in parents of certain combinations of NPA types, namely in those couples who, because of their particular genotypes, are prone to conceive non-viable progeny of either the P or null phenotype, i.e., totally lacking both traits N and A. We presume that a fetus lacking expression of both of these traits would not survive intrauterine life, appearing as a miscarriage or stillbirth, or would "fail to thrive" in early infancy.

From the genotypes given in Tables 1 and 3, it can be shown that such infertility could occur only *in the mating of a non-aggressive type with a non-sanguine type*, namely N×A, N×PA, NP×A and NP×PA. Depending on the exact genotypes of the parents, infertility on this basis could be partial or complete [*14*].

If we update Table 2 to include the possible non-viable P and null types in the offspring, the result is Table 4, below.

	N	A	NP	NA	PA	NPA
N	N NA	"	"	"	"	"
A	N NA 0 A	NA A	"	"	"	"
NP	N NP NA NPA	N NP P NA NPA PA 0 A	N NP NA NPA	"	"	"
NA	N NA	NA A	N NP NA NPA	NA	"	"
PA	N NP P NA NPA PA 0 A	NA NPA PA A	N NP P NA NPA PA 0 A	NA NPA PA A	NA NPA PA A	"
NPA	N NP NA NPA	NA NPA PA A	N NP NA NPA	NA NPA	NA NPA PA A	NA NPA
FATHER OR MOTHER	N	A	NP	NA	PA	NPA

Table 4. Possible NPA types in offspring, including the non-viable P and 0 (null) types. Encircled are possible progeny of the four parental matches that could conceive non-viable types. These marches are: N×A, N×PA, NP×A and NP×PA.

From Table 4 it follows that of the six Dominant types, *only the NA and NPA types are not vulnerable to infertile matches* by the mechanism outlined above. Because the NA and NPA Dominant types have both of the N and A traits fully expressed, they could never be a parent of a P or null phenotype.

To summarize, the NPA model directly and unavoidably calls our attention to the possibility that some parental matches of NPA types will be relatively infertile and some even completely infertile. This mechanism of infertility is limited to those matches where one parent is a non-aggressive type and the other is a non-sanguine type. The NA and NPA+ types are not vulnerable to infertile matings, irrespective of the NPA type of any matched partner.

Passive Aggressive types

Degree of inhibition of the A trait

The NPA model differentiates two subtypes of inhibited aggression in the Passive Aggressive types, corresponding to the A− and A= traits in the *non-compliant* and *compliant* types. This is more than just a theoretical subdivision, as in real life we do, indeed, observe individuals who fit the two subtypes. On the one hand, there are those individuals who are active in social relationships and can readily assume a dominant "A+" role with respect to companions. On the other hand, there are those more introverted individuals who adopt a deferential life style in virtually all interpersonal relations.

Although our model does differentiate between these contrasts of inhibited aggression, for purposes of tracing genetic traits in families we make the simplest assumption: that, in a family, only a single genetic mechanism is responsible for inhibited aggression, no matter how profound the inhibition may be. This is equivalent to an assumption that the genetic cause underlying inhibited aggression in a family is the same whether the individual has the A− or A= trait. Thus, we shall use the term "A− trait" to include various gradations of the inhibition of aggression, irrespective whether an individual in a particular family would best be described as "compliant" or "non-compliant" Passive Aggressive.

Basis of inhibited aggression in Passive Aggressive types

The genetic basis of the A− trait may turn out to be complex, as there could exist more than one gene that contributes to the inhibition of aggression in Passive Aggressive types. It is possible that the gene underlying the A− trait in one family may be different from that in another family.

Nevertheless, in our evaluation of representative families where both the A and A− traits were present, we did find a striking trend, namely a child with the trait of inhibited aggression consistently had a parent with the trait as well. That is, in these families, the A− trait was transmitted in an apparent *Mendelian dominant* mode from generation to generation.

Applying the principle of parsimony ("don't make things more complicated than they need be"), our model assumes the simplest genetic mechanism consistent with our observation: that the mechanism behind the A− trait is a modulation of trait A, rather than it being a separate, distinct trait that assorts itself independently. Thus, whether the functional A− allele is at the A locus itself or at a completely separate chromosomal locus, it follows logically that individuals who lack trait A (i.e., N or NP types) could be silent carriers of the A− trait [*15*].

Possible offspring of Passive Aggressive types

When one or both parents have the A− trait, the scheme for the inheritance of the NPA traits turns out to be only slightly more complicated than it is for Dominant types. The scheme is identical, except that the A− trait provides an "overlay" in the sense that we must consider, in addition, the possibility of A− trait in those offspring where fully-expressed trait A is predicted for the comparable Dominant type.

An illustrative example is shown in Table 5 for the possible progeny of the mating NP×NA−. The possible types in the offspring are the same as for the match of the Dominant types NP×NA, except that we must include also the possibility of A− trait in the children. Thus, for the NA×NP mating there are four possibilities for the types in the children: N, NP, NA and NPA. For the NP×NA− mating, there are two additional possibilities: NA− and NPA−.

	N	A	NP	NA	PA	NPA
N	N NA	"	"	"	"	"
A	N NA 0 A	NA A	"	"	"	"
NP	N NP NA NPA	N NP P NA NPA PA 0 A	N NP NA NPA	"	"	"
NA (NA−)	N NA	NA A	N NP NA NPA (NA− NPA−)	NA	"	"
PA	N NP P NA NPA PA 0 A	NA NPA PA A	N NP P NA NPA PA 0 A	NA NPA PA A	NA NPA PA A	"
NPA	N NP NA NPA	NA NPA PA A	N NP NA NPA	NA NPA	NA NPA PA A	NA NPA
FATHER OR MOTHER	N	A	NP	NA	PA	NPA

Table 5. NPA types in offspring when one or both parents have the A− trait. The results are the same as for the case of Dominant parents, except that we must add the possibility of A− trait in the offspring. The encircled example shows the mating NP×NA−.

Infertility in Passive Aggressive types

Infertility in the NPA model is predicted wherever there is a parental combination that is prone to conceiving progeny of the P or null genotype (Tables 3 and 4). As outlined above, in Dominant types this can occur only if one parent is a non-aggressive (N or NP) type and the other parent is a non-sanguine (A or PA) type. Parental NA and NPA types have no vulnerability to such infertile matings, irrespective of the types of their matched partners.

For an NA− or NPA− Passive Aggressive type as a parent, it can similarly be shown that there are no matings that could possibly lead to non-viable progeny of the P or null phenotype. Thus, as was the case for the Dominant NA and NPA types, the NA− and NPA− *Passive Aggressive types have no vulnerability to infertile matings*, irrespective of their matched partners.

Resigned types

Possible offspring of Resigned types

The –A trait of resignation is presumed to be caused by *environmental factors* in a mature individual who was formerly either 1) a Dominant NA or NPA type, or 2) a Passive Aggressive NA– or NPA– type. Therefore, it follows that for Resigned types we can use Tables 4 and 5 to predict the NPA types of offspring, just as we previously did for the Dominant and Passive Aggressive types.

Of course, it would be critically important to establish the correct category of the individual's "pre-resignation state". That is, one would need an accurate appraisal of the individual's behavior in early adulthood as to whether he or she was a Dominant NA or NPA+ type, or a Passive Aggressive type having the A– trait.

Infertility in Resigned types

As discussed above, Dominant NA or NPA+ types, and Passive Aggressive NA– or NPA– types, are both invulnerable to infertile matings. As the genetic mechanisms underlying Resigned types are identical to the Dominant and Passive Aggressive types, the N–A and NP–A *Resigned types similarly have no vulnerability to infertile matings*, irrespective of their matched partners.

7

Typing People

Identifying the various NPA types

As yet, there exist no objective genetic or laboratory tests for identification of the NPA traits in an individual. The best that we can do, for the time being, is to use approximate, sometimes subjective methods.

In medicine, and especially in the areas of human behavior and psychiatry, diagnoses are frequently made on subjective criteria, typically on the basis of the diagnostic opinions of physicians. One day, medical and psychological diagnoses will be made on the basis of objective testing, but we are still decades from that idealized state of affairs.

There are, nevertheless, several ways by which we can assess a person's NPA type. The ones that we consider below are: 1) by identifying specific NPA traits, 2) by *gestalt*, 3) from descriptions of an individual's appearance and behavior, 4) by identifying the N and A rages, 5) by a questionnaire, and 6) by inference from the assessed NPA types of an individual's relatives.

1. Presence of the three traits — Sometimes one can easily identify a specific trait in an individual by direct observation. For example, if one observed a child obsessively arranging toys into neat, symmetrical arrangements, one could presume that she had the P trait.

2. An individual's gestalt — We mean by *gestalt* the general impression that an individual gives in social situations, in all of the nuances of his or her physical appearance and behavior. As we observed in the character "profiles" of the previous chapters, sometimes an individual's pattern of behavior is so distinctive that it can be easily caricaturized. Hence, we can often identify the NPA type of an individual by *gestalt* alone, just as a zoologist immediately identifies a chimpanzee without focusing on any particular physical or behavioral qualities of the animal. We can identify a particular type, say an NPA+ Dominant type, in one fell swoop — all three traits at once — without our focusing on any particular aspect of any of the NPA traits.

3. Descriptions of an individual's appearance and behavior — An individual's NPA type, perhaps of someone long deceased, can also be assessed from written descriptions of behavior and from other archival information. If family lore has it that your great-grandfather convincingly fit a certain pattern, then you could propose a definite NPA type for him. For example, if he were to be described as an affable gentleman with a ruddy complexion who was a vaudeville performer, and an old photograph shows him with a broad, gingival smile, then your conjecture might be that he was an N type.

4. The N and A rages — The N or A rages may occur infrequently in a given individual, but when they do, they are typically distinctive. For example, the pallid-faced A rage in an individual of light skin color can be diagnostic of a non-sanguine A or PA type, while the vociferous, florid combined "NA rage" can be characteristic of a Dominant NPA+ type.

5. A questionnaire — Questionnaires or "personality tests" are often used in behavioral research in the absence of more scientific testing. Their limitations are well known, as there are a myriad of reasons why individuals might answer the various questions in different ways. Nevertheless, although personality questionnaires are not hard science, the results can certainly be used to generate hypotheses that could be tested and verified by other independent means, especially in the context of a family where individuals are genetically related.

We have available an online "NPA personality test" that is geared specifically to identify an individual's NPA type. The test can be used in two different ways. First, an individual can take the test directly to obtain results for his or her own NPA diagnosis. Second, the test can be used in a "surrogate" manner. That is, you can get an idea of another person's NPA type by taking the test "in their place," i.e., answering the questions like you think that he or she would answer them. Of course, you would need to know the individual very well. By this method one could even obtain an estimate of the NPA type of an individual who is long deceased, as in the case of a parent taking a "surrogate test" for a grandparent who is no longer alive.

6. By inference from the NPA types of relatives — Sometimes the model itself can assist in advancing a hypothetical or confirmatory diagnosis of an individual's NPA traits or type. For example, if it is unequivocal that both of a child's parents are sanguine, one can conjecture that the child — sight unseen — likewise has the N trait.

How accurate can NPA typing be?

There are several categories of ways by which the typing of an individual may be problematic:

The NPA model itself — The premise of our method of analyzing the heritability of personality is that the NPA model is basically correct. However, in the field of genetics complicating factors often present themselves in what are called *polygenic inheritance* and *genetic heterogeneity*. In simple terms, this means that 1) there may be several genes, rather than just a single one, underlying a trait, and 2) a trait caused by genes in one family can be mimicked by a different set of genes in another family. As yet, we do not have evidence that such possible complications are relevant to the NPA model, but we should be aware of this possibility.

Biological variability — As we emphasized in Chapter 2, although an individual may be distinctly male or female, or of a particular discrete NPA type, every individual has an overlay of behavioral complexity in the categories of "other genes" and environment. Although it is almost always easy to identify a person's gender, it may require some investigation — and sometimes sleuthing — to acquire enough relevant information to establish a definite NPA diagnosis with which one is comfortable.

Typing individuals in a particular family — The ease with which one can type individuals will necessarily vary from family to family, depending on how many individuals there are, on their NPA diagnoses, how they are related, the amount and quality of information that exists with regard to their physical appearance and behavior, and finally, on how much experience the investigating individual has had in using the NPA model.

In general, one should use all available information, including that related to family members who are deceased. One should be aware that questions of paternity may arise, and one may need to decide at some point whether one's analysis is something that could be shared with other family members or is something that is best kept private.

8

Parents and Offspring:
Case Studies

We are now ready to tackle the ultimate question: given a set of parents in a particular family, to what extent can we predict the possible NPA types of the offspring?

As we shall see, sometimes the answer is straightforward and clear, but this is not always so. In other situations, there may be subtle features of NPA inheritance that will demand our attention.

"The Table"

The basis for our analyses of specific examples of parental combinations is the table that we derived in Chapter 6 for "Possible NPA phenotypes in offspring." For convenience, it is reproduced overleaf as Table 6. We shall refer to it as "the Table".

To summarize, the features of the Table are:

- It displays all possible types of the progeny on the assumption that the parental genotypes are unknown.

- It includes the possible non-viable P and null phenotypes.

- Although it was derived for Dominant types, it may also be applied to Passive Aggressive and Resigned types by adding the A− trait to the types of the progeny, where applicable.

	N	A	NP	NA	PA	NPA
N	N NA	"	"	"	"	"
A	N NA 0 A	NA A	"	"	"	"
NP	N NP NA NPA	N NP P NA NPA PA 0 A	N NP NA NPA	"	"	"
NA	N NA	NA A	N NP NA NPA	NA	"	"
PA	N NP P NA NPA PA 0 A	NA NPA PA A	N NP P NA NPA PA 0 A	NA NPA PA A	NA NPA PA A	"
NPA	N NP NA NPA	NA NPA PA A	N NP NA NPA	NA NPA	NA NPA PA A	NA NPA
FATHER OR MOTHER	N	A	NP	NA	PA	NPA

Table 6. "The Table": Possible NPA types in offspring, including the non-viable P and 0 (null) types.

General rules pertaining to the Table

On the basis of the model, with the P trait being Mendelian dominant and the N and A traits being recessive, we can state the following general rules:

- If both parents have the N trait, then all children must also have the N trait. That is, if both parents are "sanguine", all children must be sanguine.

- If both parents have the A trait, then all children must also have the A trait. That is, if both parents are "aggressive", all children must be aggressive.

- If both parents lack the P trait, then all children must also lack the P trait. That is, if both parents are "non-perfectionistic", all children must be non-perfectionistic.

Or conversely, the rules are:

- A non-sanguine child (who lacks the N trait) must have a parent who is also non-sanguine.

- A non-aggressive child (who lacks the A trait) must have a parent who is also non-aggressive.

- A perfectionistic child (who has the P trait) must have a parent who is also perfectionistic.

With regard to infertility, the rules are:

- Non-viable progeny can occur only if one parent is a non-sanguine type and the other is non-aggressive type.

- Neither the NA type nor the NPA+ type can be the parent of a non-viable type.

With regard to the "silent" carrier state:

- If a sanguine child has a non-sanguine parent, the parent must be a carrier of the recessive allele **n**.

- If an aggressive child has a non-aggressive parent, the parent must be a carrier of the recessive allele **a**.

- If a non-sanguine child has a sanguine parent, the child must be a carrier of the recessive allele **n**.

- If a non-aggressive child has an aggressive parent, the child must be a carrier of the recessive allele **a**.

Some additional conditions are:

- Parents can have children of their own NPA type, but a child's NPA type need not be the same as either parent.

- The NA type can arise in the progeny of any two parental phenotypes.

- The Table assumes no specific knowledge of the genotypes in the parents. In a specific case, where the genotypes of the parents are known, the possibilities of the NPA types of the offspring may be more limited than those shown.

Examples

We present below illustrative examples of inheritance according to the NPA model. We consider, in order of complexity, first cases of Dominant parents, then Passive Aggressive, and finally Resigned types.

Dominant types

Case 1. When the parents are both of the same NPA type, what can we say about the offspring?

If both parents are of the same type, the six possibilities are those shown along the diagonal of Table 6, as follows:

Parents	Possible Children
N × N	N, NA
A × A	A, NA
NA × NA	NA
NP × NP	N, NA, NP, NPA
PA × PA	A, NA, PA, NPA
NPA × NPA	NA, NPA

Note that there is only one possibility for the NA×NA match. In fact, of all the NPA types, the NA type is the only one that always "breeds true". That is, any two NA types will always have offspring only of the NA type. This occurs because the NA type is the only type that has just a single possible genotype, namely the fully homozygous **(nnaa)**.

Comment: If we lack further information regarding the NPA types of related individuals in these matches, then all of the above possibilities must be considered in any particular case.

Case 2. Giovanni, an NPA+ entrepreneur of Italian heritage marries Pania, a Polynesian lady of the N type. What are the possibilities in the children?

From the Table, the possibilities are N, NA, NP and NPA.

Case 3. Giovanni and Pania have a long and fruitful marriage, with an issue of six sons and eight daughters. It turns out that all of the children are NP types. What's going on?

This could occur only if 1) Giovanni was homozygous for the P trait, and 2) Pania was not a carrier of the recessive **a** allele of the A trait. Thus, the genotypes of these two individuals must be: Giovanni: **(nnPPaa)** and Pania: **(nn)**, and it follows that all of the children must be of genotype **(nnPa)**. Thus, all of the children are silent carriers of the recessive **a** allele.

Furthermore, since Giovanni is homozygous for the P trait, this means that both of his parents must have had the P trait, as well. Similarly, since Pania is not a carrier of the A trait, this means that neither of her parents had the A trait. They must have been either N or NP types

Comment: This is an example of how analysis of *phenotypes* in related individuals can allow one to determine their *genotypes*.

Case 4. Giovanni, now a retired widower, has become smitten with Delilah, an actress of the NA type. They are going to have an illegitimate child. What are the possibilities in the child?

From the Table, the possibilities in the children of a NPA×NA union are: NA and NPA. However, we know from Case 3 that Giovanni is homozygous for the P trait, having the genotype **(nnPPaa)**. For her part, Delilah can be only of genotype **(nnaa)**. Therefore, the child, as yet unborn, must be of the NPA+ phenotype, having genotype **(nnPaa)**.

Comment: There is no possibility that this child will have the NA phenotype of the mother.

Case 5. Upset by her father's intemperate behavior, and not thinking very clearly, Rosalina, third daughter of Giovanni and Pania, marries Igor, a Russian Mafioso, clearly of the A type. What are the possibilities in their children?

From the Table, the possibilities in the children of a NP×A mating are all six Dominant types: N, A, NA, NP, PA and NPA. Also, the non-viable P and null types are possible, so this is a union that is subject to at least partial infertility (miscarriages, stillbirth, etc.). We know that the union is not subject to *complete* infertility, since Rosalina is a silent carrier of the **a** allele. That is, at least some of the progeny will have fully expressed A trait.

We know from Case 3 that Rosalina's genotype is **(nnPa)**. Igor's genotype must be either **(aa)** or **(naa)**. If it is the latter, then all six of the Dominant types are possible in the children. If it is the former, then the children's types could only be the non-sanguine types A or PA.

Comment: This is an example of partial infertility. In a case of complete infertility, all of the progeny would be of only the P or null phenotypes.

Case 6. Bogdan, a PA type, marries Lulu, an NA type. They intend to have a very large family. Could all of the children be non-sanguine PA types, like the father? Could they all be sanguine NA types, like the mother?

From the Table, the four possibilities of the types in the children of all PA×NA unions are: A, NA, PA and NPA. Nevertheless, it is possible for all of the children to be of PA type in a particular match. This could occur here if Bogdan was 1) homozygous for the P trait, and 2) not a carrier of the recessive **n** allele. That is, Bogdan's genotype would need to be **(PPaa)**, which could occur only if both of Bogdan's parents were non-sanguine PA types as well.

However, there is virtually *no* possibility that a large number of children would all be NA types like the mother, since at least fifty percent of the children would receive the father's dominant P trait.

Case 7. Bogdan and Lulu have just had their first child, and it is an NA type. What can they expect for their future large family?

As the first child is an NA type, necessarily of genotype **(nnaa)**, this means that in actuality Bogdan must be of genotype **(nPaa)**. That is, he must be a carrier of the recessive allele **n** and also heterozygous for the **P** allele. If one works out the probabilities for the possible NPA types of the children, the result is that the four types A, NA, PA and NPA are all equally probable.

Comment: This will be a very heterogeneous family from the point of view of personality.

Note: To calculate the probability of a particular NPA type in the progeny, one multiplies together the three individual probabilities of having (or not having) the traits N, P and A according to the various possible combinations of alleles received in random fashion from the mother and father.

Case 8. Catrine is an NP type from a Scandinavian family. Not only is she an NP type, but "all of her family for generations have been NP types". Now, living in the USA, she dreams of having a child "with a personality just like mine," and is planning pregnancy by means of artificial insemination via an unknown donor. What are the chances that the child will have the desired NP type?

Surprisingly, the chances are excellent. Maybe even close to a sure thing.

If, indeed, everyone in the family has been of the NP type for generations, then Catrine's genotype is highly likely **(nnPP)**. This genotype means that whatever be the genotype of the potential father, the progeny 1) cannot have the A trait, and 2) must have the P trait. In short, among the viable types, only the NP type is possible in the child.

If the sperm donor happened to be a non-sanguine A or PA type, then the progeny would be either NP type or non-viable. The risk of non-viability (miscarriage, etc.) would be at least fifty percent. For some non-sanguine sperm donors, for example a PA type with the genotype **(PPaa)**, *all* progeny would be non-viable P types, and no viable children could ever come from that particular donor match.

Comment: The latter instance of the non-sanguine sperm donor would be an example of a match characterized by *complete infertility.*

Case 9. Fayrah is an NA type from the Middle East, and a friend of Catrine's (Case 8). She is delighted by the success that Catrine has had in mothering a child of her own personality type. Fayrah similarly states that "all of her family for generations have been NA types." She, too, dreams of having a child "with a personality just like mine," and

likewise plans pregnancy by means of artificial insemination via a random donor. What are the chances that the child will have the desired NA type?

Not very high.

Fayrah's genotype can be only **(nnaa)**, irrespective of her heritage, so the fact that she comes from a long line of NA types is irrelevant. In order for the child to also be an NA type, the child must receive from the donor father 1) an **n** allele, *and* 2) no **P** allele, *and* 3) an **a** allele. That is a very tall order.

If the donor happened to be an NA type, then of course the child would have to be the desired NA type as well. However, in most areas of the USA, NA types are in the small minority, so this is not especially likely. A look at the Table shows that in matings of an NA type with other ("non-NA") types, all of the viable types are possible in the progeny. On the average, it is no more likely that the child will have the mother's desired NA phenotype than the father's undesired type, along with all of the other undesired types. Thus, the probability of the child's being an NA type is at best on the order of 50-50, and probably much lower, given that the P trait is common in the USA.

Comment: In this case, there is no worry about infertility (possible miscarriage, etc.) because an NA type is invulnerable to having non-viable progeny of the P or null type, irrespective of the NPA type of the father.

Case 10. Natalie and Nathan are non-identical twins who were separated at birth and raised in foster homes. They now meet and discover that they are NP and PA types, respectively. What can we say about their parents?

As can be deduced from the Table, this could occur only if one of the parents was a non-aggressive N or NP type, and the other was a non-sanguine A or PA type. At least one of the parents would need to have the P trait. The non-aggressive parent would need to have been a carrier of the **a** allele, while the non-sanguine parent would need to have been a carrier of the **n** allele.

Comment: The parental match here is another instance of partial infertility. Since both parents are carriers of the recessive

a and **n** alleles, we can calculate that on the average one out of four of their pregnancies would result in a non-viable P or null type. That is, such a union could expect a miscarriage rate of 25 percent.

Case 11. Lucien and Brigitte were students when they first met at a French university. They discover that they have common interests, and indeed that they are both NP types. They eventually marry, intending to have a large family of quiet, well-behaved children. To their consternation, their first child is a rambunctious NA type! Could this happen? Lucien would not in a million years suspect that Brigitte was unfaithful to him.

Yes, it could happen. From the Table, we can see that the possibilities of a NP×NP union are: N, NP, NA and NPA. If the first child is an NA type, this means that Lucien and Brigitte are both carriers of the **a** allele, and both have the genotype **(nnPa)**. If one works out the probabilities for the possible NPA types of the children, one finds that the four types would occur, respectively, in the relative ratio of NA:N:NPA:NP = 1:3:3:9.

Comment: Although Lucien and Brigitte's first child was an NA type, the odds of this happening is only 1 in 16. Their hope of having a family of quiet, well-behaved NP children is not likely to be fulfilled, as almost one-half of the children will be N, NA and NPA types.

Other combinations of NP×NP matings (i.e., different genotypes) could yield 1) all NP types, 2) only NP and N types, or 3) only NP and NPA types. It is not possible for the offspring to be only NP and NA types.

France is a polymorphic society from the point of view of NPA type, with NP types being in the minority. Thus, it is not unreasonable that NP types in such a society would be silent carriers of the **a** allele, as Lucien and Brigitte were in this case.

Case 12. A lady of a certain age, wearing a long red dress and too much lipstick, appears on the scene. She appears to be a somewhat starry-eyed N type. She claims to be Olga, the long-lost daughter of Prince Dmitri Roshav-Polovskii, who was

cruelly exiled in 1947. When it is pointed out to her that it is common knowledge that the Prince and his wife were both non-sanguine types, Olga replies, "Yes, I know. I researched that, and I read that it is possible for non-sanguine parents to have a sanguine child". Is "Olga" telling the truth, or is she an impostora?

She is an *impostora*.

Although two non-sanguine types can have a sanguine child, they cannot have a child of the N type. Non-sanguine types have the A trait, so all of the progeny of two non-sanguine parents must have the A trait as well.

Case 13. Scarlett, a business executive and mother of three, is an NA type. Against her better judgment, she has a prolonged intimate affair with her immediate boss, Wolf, who is a dynamic, managerial-autocratic NPA+ type. Scarlett becomes pregnant and eventually bears a child, who turns out to be an NP type. What has happened here?

From the Table, it is apparent that an NP child could not be the result of an NA×NPA union. Hence, Wolf could not possibly be the father of the child.

Also, from the Table it can be seen that in order for an NA type to be the mother of an NP child, the father would have to be an NP type as well. If Scarlett's husband were an NP type, the issue would be resolved, and we could rest our case.

Comment: Sometimes the results of a family analysis are best kept private.

Case 14. Spike and Nora are both NA types who are about to have a child. Spike's parents are NP×NPA, while Nora's parents are N×PA. The forthcoming child's expectant grandparents (who are very different from each other in personality) are each secretly hoping that the child's personality type will be "just like mine." What are the chances that the child will have the same NPA type as one of the grandparents?

The chances are zero.

As the Table shows, the child's type can only be NA type. The mating of any two NA types can produce offspring only of the NA type. Knowledge of the types of the grandparents, although interesting, is not relevant to the determination of the type of the grandchild.

Comment: The NA type is the only type that always "breeds true."

Passive Aggressive types

Case 15. When the parents are both Passive Aggressive types, what can we say about the offspring?

If both parents have the A− trait, the possibilities in the offspring are those previously shown in Table 6 for the NA and NPA Dominant types, except we must add the possibility of A− trait in the offspring, as follows:

Parents	Possible Children
NA− × NA−	NA, NA−
NA− × NPA−	NA, NA−, NPA, NPA−
NPA− × NPA−	NA, NA−, NPA, NPA−

Comment: Note that when two parents are both Passive Aggressive types, a child can nevertheless be a Dominant NA or NPA+ type.

Case 16. When the parents are both Passive Aggressive types, what is the probability that a child will be of a Dominant type?

The probability of a child's being a Dominant type (i.e., NA or NPA+) is the product of the probabilities of not receiving the A− trait from either parent, or $\frac{1}{2} \times \frac{1}{2} = \frac{1}{4}$. That is, the probability of a child's being a Dominant type is 25 percent, and a Passive Aggressive type 75 percent.

Comment: The above assumes the uncomplicated situation where each parent has just a single dose of inherited A− trait.

Case 17. Nigel and Heather are both NPA− types. Their first child is an NA− type. What can they expect if they have a large family?

From Case 15 above, the possibilities of the progeny in all matings of NPA− × NPA− are: NA, NA−, NPA and NPA−. In the case of Nigel and Heather, the fact that the first child lacks the P trait means that neither parent is homozygous for the **P** allele, hence that all four of the types listed are possible in the offspring.

If one works out the probabilities for the possible NPA types of the children, one finds that the four types NA, NA−, NPA and NPA− would occur, respectively, in the relative ratio of 1:3:3:9.

Case 18. The medieval monarch, King Lucifer IV was an NA− type known for his profligacy with many mistresses of the NA type and for siring many illegitimate children. The king's parents were first cousins. According to the chronicles of the time, the king's illegitimate children were all NA− types, without exception. Could this really happen?

Yes, it could happen.

Given that the king's parents were first cousins, the king could have received a double dose of the A− trait from both his father and mother. That is, the king would have been homozygous for the "a- allele" underlying the A− trait in this family, and he would have necessarily transmitted the trait to all of his children.

Comment: In this case it is immaterial whether we assume that the homozygous condition **(a-a-)** is at the A locus, or at an entirely separate gene in a different chromosomal location. If it were at a different location, the process by which trait A could be inhibited by a separate gene is called in genetics "epistasis".

Case 19. We meet Matthias in a local bar in Rio. He tells us, in a monotone voice, the story that he is a staid NP type from the Old Country. Although he was hoping to have a quiet family life, he nevertheless, married Ana Luiza, an NA type of Iberian heritage. He tells us that his first child was an NA type, and now his second child is an NA− type! Could this really happen? If so, what can Matthias and Ana Luiza expect if they have a large family?

Yes, it could happen.

It could happen if Matthias was a carrier of the A trait, as well as a carrier of the A− trait at a different genetic locus. We have no information regarding his parentage, but he could have inherited the alleles corresponding to the two traits if one of his parents was, for example, an NA− or NPA− type.

From the Table, the possibilities of the progeny in all matings of NP×NA are: N, NP, NA and NPA, to which we must add the possibilities of NA− and NPA−. In the case of Matthias and Ana Luiza, the fact that they have a child lacking the P trait means that neither parent is homozygous for the **P** allele, hence that all six of the types listed above are possible in the offspring.

If one works out the probabilities for the possible NPA types of the children, one finds that the six types N, NP, NA, NA−, NPA and NPA− would occur, respectively, in the relative ratio of 2:2:1:1:1:1.

Comment: To explain the inhibition of trait A in this family, we added a fourth locus to the NPA model, by which the mechanism of inhibition is one of "epistasis". This was done because in this mating Matthias can transmit *three* variations of the A trait to his children: 1) fully expressed A trait, 2) inhibited trait A−, and 3) absence of A trait. An explanation of this on the basis of a single genetic locus, having only two possible alleles, would be unnecessarily complicated.

Case 20. Zoey, a well-respected NPA− investigative reporter for the New York Times, has a wild, wild affair with Effinem, an A type and the lead singer of the rock group, Tatoo Bunz. Soon, she finds herself expectant of a child. What are the possibilities of the type of the child? Which type is most probable?

From the Table, the possibilities of the progeny in all matings of NPA×A are: A, NA, PA and NPA, to which we must add the possibility of this child's inheriting the A− trait. Thus, we have four additional possibilities: A−, NA− PA− and NPA−.

Of special note here are the two types predicted by the model: A− and PA−. These types are also Passive Aggressive types, in that they carry the A− trait. However, they are also *Borderline types* because they have neither trait N nor A fully expressed. In the NPA model, Borderline types are withdrawn, "schizoid" individuals who do not speak very much and who are relatively avoidant of social interactions. We include these Borderline types here because they are an unavoidable result of the NPA model. Although in this book we have not considered the eventuality of Borderline types as parents, we cannot ignore them here as possible offspring.

We cannot say which type is the most probable in this case because we have no information as to the genotypes of either Zoey or Effinem. If the child turned out to be an NA type, then Zoey's genotype would have to be **(nnPaa-)** and Effinem's **(naa)**. In that case, all of the above eight types, including the two Borderline types, would have been possible, in equal probability.

Comment: We will return to the issue of Borderline types in the final chapter.

Resigned types

Case 21. When the parents are both Resigned types, what can we say about the offspring?

If both parents have the −A trait, the possibilities in the offspring are the same as those shown previously in Table 6 for the NA×NPA Dominant matching, except we must add the possibility of A− trait in the offspring, as follows:

Parents	Possible Children
N−A × N−A	NA, NA−
N−A × NP−A	NA, NA−, NPA, NPA−
NP−A × NP−A	NA, NA−, NPA, NPA−

Comment: The above assumes that the genotypes of the parents are unknown. That is, it includes the possibilities that each of the parents was formerly either a Dominant type or Passive Aggressive type.

Case 22. Mortimer, formerly director of the complaint department of a large haberdashery, is now the keeper of a lighthouse on the North Atlantic Coast. He says the he "got tired of being bullied all of his life and just wants to be left alone." Nevertheless, he is seduced by Brunhilde, an NA

exchange student doing research on seagulls. Nine months later she delivers of a child, who turns out to be an NPA− type. Any comment on this relationship?

Having chosen a life of quiet independence after years of apparently "playing the game" of dominance and submission, Mortimer does seems to satisfy the criteria of a Resigned type.

As the child is an NPA− type, with the mother being an NA type, this means that Mortimer must have been an NPA− type as well. Although the A− trait can be well camouflaged by the −A state of resignation, its genetic basis persists for the duration of an individual's life, as attested here by its reemergence in the life of Mortimer's child.

9

Conclusion

It's your turn

The illustrative cases of the previous chapter were presented as a representative slice of the various kinds of NPA inheritance that can occur in the real world. Now that you have worked through the cases and understand, in principle, where the numbers come from, you should be ready to tackle your own slice of life... and in particular, the case of your own family. For that purpose, we have provided in Appendix B space where you can start a list of individuals from your own personal experience, according to your diagnoses of their NPA types.

As the saying goes, truth is often stranger than fiction, and case studies from your own experience may well rival the vignettes that we presented in the previous chapter. If eventually you find that you have put together analyses that might be of interest to others, and you would like to share them, then this can easily be done [*16*].

Facing NPA reality

An intrusive model

If, on the one hand, you are new to the NPA model, then it is natural that you should feel a bit disconcerted. You may feel that the model is a bit intrusive into your daily life, as it continually nags you to provide explanations of present and bygone relationships in a new light. You may have the vague feeling that some events might be better off relegated to your subconscious mind, rather than being analyzed in the unforgiving light of day. You may feel that some past relationships might be too painful to revisit.

If, on the other hand, you are not new to the model, then you can reassure those who are that the satisfaction of appreciating the truth is almost always preferable to the bliss of ignorance.

An inconvenient model

There is no doubt about it: the NPA model raises some troublesome issues that, sooner or later, we will have to face.

From one point of view, the model is a dispassionate, predictive mathematical tool, with all of the NPA types appearing as equal players in this game of the random assortment genetic traits. The model shows no favoritism in predicting results for offspring, whether they be Dominant types, Passive Aggressive types, Borderline types, or whether they be the non-viable P and null types. The model simply rolls the dice and tells us what the possibilities could be, and — if you believe the model — what the eventualities actually will be.

However, as much as we would like to ignore it, the model does throw some cold water into our faces.

First of all, it predicts that some combinations of parental couples are vulnerable to having *non-viable progeny*. This means that some women will be subject to the risks of pregnancies in which there is no hope that the child will survive to maturity. We should emphasize that this prediction of the model is not just a vague "possibility" in these couples. It is as much of a sure thing as the prediction of any of the viable NPA types. Why should humans have evolved with a mechanism of procreation that predictably exposes women to the risk of non-viable pregnancy?

Secondly, the model predicts that some combinations of parents will have *Borderline types* among the offspring. Borderline types, such as the Passive Aggressive types A− or PA−, are "borderline" in the sense that they are very close to having no expression of either the N or A traits, as in the non-viable types. Again, the model's prediction of Borderline types is dispassionate and as much a sure thing as its prediction of any of the other types.

Just as in the case of children with Down's syndrome (who have an extra chromosome), our subjective view — and we hope, the modern view — is that all individuals, including Borderline types, have rights, and that no individuals should be considered to be "better" than any others on the basis of their underlying genetics. All individuals have their own particular limitations, and foibles, and all individuals need assistance from others sometime during their lives, especially when they are very young or very old.

Nevertheless, in a very stark manner, the model predicts the occurrence of Borderline types, who are individuals that many would describe as "mentally handicapped" in our modern society. It is as if the All-knowing Model, in dispensing decks of genetic cards to developing fetuses, says to a Borderline type, "Sorry, you don't get a full deck." Why should humans have evolved with a mechanism of procreation in which some children are predictably placed at such a disadvantage in a world where only the fittest are meant to survive?

Finally, the NPA model threatens to bring us into a Brave New World in which individuals are coldly classified according to their genetic types, raising so many issues that it is difficult to venture which ones are the most important.

But if this is beginning to give you a headache, there is a final option, and here it is. Just close your eyes, clench your hands very tightly, and hope — hope really, really hard — that it is all not true.

APPENDICES

APPENDIX A

NPA PERSONALITY THEORY: SYNOPSIS
Personality theory based on the genetic traits of sanguinity, perfectionism and aggression

The NPA theory of personality was developed by A.M. Benis on the basis of concepts presented over fifty years ago by psychiatrist Karen Horney. The model posits three major behavioral traits underlying personality: sanguinity (N), perfectionism (P) and aggression (A), leading to the formulation of discrete character types. Each trait is based on a major pleiotropic gene (a gene determining several related characteristics) that follows the rules of Mendelian genetics.

The NPA model proposes that the character traits A and N are indispensable to human development, being related to the sympathetic and parasympathetic nervous systems, respectively. The trait P is also assumed to function at the level of the central nervous system and to act as a modifier of the expression of traits A and N. The NPA model proposes to clarify the genetic bases of known personality disorders, diseases related to behavioral factors ("psychosomatic diseases") and mental illnesses.

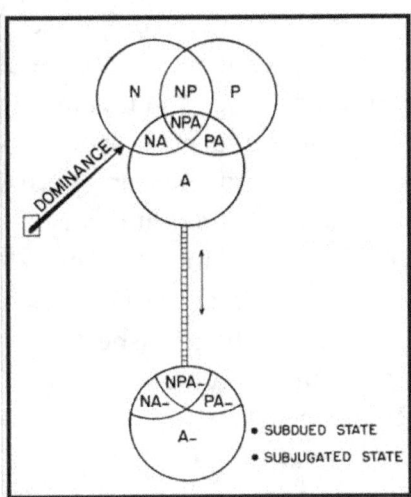

Fig. A1. Venn diagram of Dominant character types. Character types having the trait of aggression A may be reduced, reversibly, to a subdued or subjugated state A–.

Contents

What is personality?

Psychologists speak of personality as "a collection of emotional, thought and behavioral patterns unique to a person that is consistent over time" [1]. Although many investigators have proposed various theories of personality, no objectively testable model has emerged. The NPA model falls into the category of a trait theory of personality, its unique approach being that it is biologically based on classical human genetics.

NPA model based on three genetic traits

Genetics and environment

Although it is universally accepted that both genetic and environmental factors (or "nature and nurture") comprise personality, the relevant genes have yet to be identified [2]. Studies of the heritability of personality factors conducted with identical and fraternal twins emphasize the importance of genetics in behavior [3]. The NPA model acknowledges the possible importance of environment and culture in personality but emphasizes that it is the genetic, or structural, factors that first need to be identified.

The NPA model acknowledges that the genetic bases of personality are themselves complex. It assumes at least four tiers to this genetic basis:

- male or female gender

- character type based on the three NPA traits

- temperament, or the degree of activity or excitability of an individual in the Pavlovian sense

- other facets of personality, such as Raymond Cattell's 16 Personality Factors or Hans Eysenck's P-E-N model of personality.

The NPA model, thus, focuses on only the second of these four tiers, acknowledging that temperament and other facets of personality may involve a large number of genes.

Fig. A2. Karen Horney (1885-1952)

Traits of sanguinity, perfectionism and aggression

Karen Horney advanced the concept that at maturity there exist at least three expansive character types, namely the "narcissistic", the "perfectionistic" and the "arrogant-vindictive" [5]. Extending these ideas, the NPA model posits that the human character rests primarily on the existence of three major traits: sanguinity (N), perfectionism (P) and aggression (A). Each of these traits is assumed to exist as the expression of a single major pleiotropic gene. Horney considered that the traits have environmental origins, being the result of an individual's desperate search for dominance in the context of a stifling upbringing [5]. The NPA model — in ascribing the traits to genetic origins — emphasizes biological attributes associated with the traits.

Aggression (A)

The behavioral trait of aggression is proposed to be the most labile of the three [6]. The stereotypic acts associated with this trait involve body posturing, gestures, and eye contact of intimidation and deference, with individuals having this trait continually competing with each other on a scale of dominance and submission. The trait of aggression corresponds to a striving for *power* over one's environment, hence it is one main component of competitiveness in social relations, or ambition. In a pejorative connotation the trait may reveal itself in the context of sadism or sadomasochism. The facial expression is non-sanguine, i.e., tending toward sallowness or pallor in individuals of light skin color. The hallmark of the trait of aggression is a mass discharge of the sympathetic nervous system: the "flight or fight" response or the aggressive-vindictive rage. During the expression of this rage, the facial complexion of pallor is accentuated.

Sanguinity (N)

The trait of sanguinity (Horney's "narcissism") is proposed to be less labile than that of aggression (where individuals may be constantly altering their character states on a scale of dominance and submission) [6]. The stereotypic acts associated with the trait include self-flaunting body posturing, expansive arm gestures, bowing, instinctive self-adornment, and a natural attraction to the limelight of personal recognition. Individuals having only this trait (of the three) are competitive but non-aggressive in their strivings for recognition. The trait corresponds to a striving for *glory* in one's environment, representing the second main component of human ambition. In the absence of mediating factors, the unbridled trait of sanguinity may reveal itself in the context of conceit, exhibitionism, vanity or messianism. An associated facial expression includes the radiant gingival smile (broadly exposing the gums and teeth). The facial complexion in individuals of light skin color tends toward blood-red or ruddy. Hallmarks of the trait include blushing, flushing, and a mass discharge of the autonomic nervous system: the narcissistic rage of defense and withdrawal. During expression of this rage the normally sanguine complexion becomes even more florid.

Perfectionism (P)

The trait of perfectionism in the NPA model is not a basic drive of ambition and is not associated with a rage reaction [6]. Rather it is a mediator of the unbridled drives of aggression and/or sanguinity. The stereotypic acts associated with the trait of perfectionism are obsessiveness, compulsiveness, repetition, and the maintenance of neatness, order and symmetry. A clue to the nature of the trait lies in the compulsive, repetitive mannerisms of autistic children and some adult schizophrenic individuals. The behavioral pattern is often ritualistic and the speech characterized by echolalia. It is posited that such autistic and schizophrenic individuals are those in whom the two components of ambition, i.e., aggression and sanguinity, have been suppressed by genetic or environmental factors, either congenitally, in childhood, or after maturity, thus revealing in the individual a primitive state of perfectionism.

Character types

The notion that humans exhibit only a limited number of discrete character types can be traced back to the time of the ancient Greeks, in particular to the theory of humors (blood, black bile, yellow bile and phlegm). The NPA model attempts to relate genetic NPA types to these character types of antiquity, as well as to the classic personality disorders of modern psychiatry.

Fig. A3. Character types according to the ancient theory of humors: *Phlegmaticus, Cholericus, Sanguineus* and *Melancholicus. [J.K. Lavater, ca. 1775]*

Dominance: Dominant character types

In Dominant types the traits A and N, if present at all, are fully expressed [6]. The NPA model generates the following character types:

N type

The *sanguine (N) type* is found in the writings of Horney [7] and others who have developed the classic psychiatric views of narcissism. In the NPA model this type is the equivalent of the sanguine character type described by the ancients. The important attributes of this type are: expansiveness but unaggressiveness, non-perfectionism, a tendency to flamboyant self-adornment, a natural attraction to the limelight, the gingival smile of recognition and the florid narcissistic rage. In extreme forms this type appears as a self-anointed visionary, a proselytizing evangelist or a messianic personality.

A type

The *aggressive (A) type* corresponds to Horney's arrogant-vindictive type and to her concept of "moving against people" [8]. In the NPA model this is the classic choleric character type of antiquity. The main attributes of this type are: unbridled arrogance, instinctual vindictiveness, non-perfectionism, no tendency to self-adornment, a wry or sardonic grin in place of a gingival smile, and the pallid-complexioned aggressive-vindictive rage. In extreme forms this type appears as a sadistic personality, as an extroverted paranoid personality, or as the so-called antisocial or sociopathic personality.

NA type

The *sanguine-aggressive (NA) type* is regarded to be a composite of the previously described sanguine and aggressive types. Horney described the essence of this character type, in the female, in an article, "The overvaluation of love: a study of a common present day type" [9]. The main attributes of this type are: a sanguine complexion, synergistic merging of unbridled narcissism and aggression, hyperactivity, non-perfectionism, a tendency toward extreme self-adornment, exhibitionism in the limelight, a "flashy" extroverted smile and a tendency toward aggressive-vindictive or combined narcissistic-aggressive rages. In extreme forms this type appears as the hypomanic, histrionic or hysterical personality.

NP type

The attributes of the *sanguine-perfectionist (NP) type* were described by Horney in her exposition of the "perfectionist type" [4]. In the NPA model this encompasses the classic phlegmatic type known to the ancients. The main qualities of this type are: a tendency toward a sanguine complexion, industriousness, orderliness, an intense sense of duty, unaggressiveness, stubbornness, negativism, a tendency to ruminate, perfectionistic rather than unbridled self-adornment, an uncommonly seen gingival smile of recognition, and the capacity to exhibit the florid narcissistic rage. In extreme forms this character appears as the obsessive-compulsive personality.

PA type

The *perfectionistic-aggressive (PA)* type is alluded to by Horney in her mention of aggressive types who function in the capacity of a "power behind the throne" [8], that is, personages who utilize intellectual qualities and planning rather than overt aggression to achieve their aims. In the NPA model this is the classic non-sanguine, austere melancholic personality of the ancients. The principal qualities of this type are: a non-sanguine complexion, passive-aggressive behavior, dour perfectionism, vigilance, manipulativeness, a proud bearing, haughty reservedness, a calculated vindictiveness, a lack of an innate tendency to self-adornment, a sardonic grin, and the pallid aggressive-vindictive rage. In extreme forms this is the passive-aggressive, rebellious-distrustful, or ruminating paranoid personality.

NPA type

The *sanguine-perfectionistic-aggressive (NPA) type* was not explicitly described by Horney, although she did note that the three traits can coexist in the same individual [10]. The main attributes of this type are: a sanguine complexion, a loud voice, dynamism with a tendency to be overbearing, bombastic garrulity, intense eye contact, a strong sense of duty, a bent toward conventional values, unpretentious self-adornment, an outgoing smile of moderate intensity, and the capacity to exhibit the narcissistic, aggressive, or explosive narcissistic-aggressive rages. In the extreme cases this individual is the managerial-autocratic or explosive personality.

Submission: Passive Aggressive character types

In Passive Aggressive types the trait of aggression is not fully expressed [6]. The NPA model defines two gradations of relative submission: *non-compliance*, in which the individual is basically submissive but is easily activated to an energetic state of aggression, and *compliance*, in which the individual tends to remain in a profound state of submission.

In the model the state of submission, or inhibition of aggression, most often has a genetic basis, the result of a congenital, incomplete expression of the gene for the trait A. However, the model also allows for environmental causes, the state of submission being induced during the juvenile period on the basis of environmental constraints to character development. That is, phenocopies (based on environmental factors) of a genetically disposed submissive state may exist. Also, like Dominant types having full expression of the trait A, Passive Aggressive types may exhibit the aggressive A rage.

Non-compliant types

The model denotes the state of non-compliance by A–, obtaining the following *non-compliant* phenotypes:

- **Aggressive (A–)**
- **Perfectionistic-aggressive (PA–)**
- **Sanguine (NA–)**
- **Sanguine-perfectionistic (NPA–)**

Compliant types

The model denotes the state of compliance by A=, obtaining the following *compliant* phenotypes:

- **Aggressive (A=)**
- **Perfectionistic-aggressive (PA=)**
- **Sanguine (NA=)**
- **Sanguine-perfectionistic (NPA=)**

The *NPA– non-compliant type* above corresponds to active, motivated, non-confrontational individuals whose baseline personality tends toward submissiveness, as described by Horney in her discussion of "inverted sadistic" behavior [11]. In the therapeutic setting, these individuals are found over the spectrum of the "Type A", dependent, and phobic-anxious personality. The *NA– type* is a non-perfectionistic, active individual, often exhibiting unbridled narcissistic behavior. In the therapeutic setting this is a cyclothymic or dependent histrionic personality.

The *compliant types NA=* and *NPA=* above correspond to more profoundly submissive individuals, having more pronounced tendencies toward masochistic behavior [12]. They correspond to Horney's compliant "self-effacing" personality and to her concept of "moving toward people" [13].

Resignation: Resigned character types

In the character state of resignation, the trait of aggression is stunted after maturity because of environmental constraints [6]. Unlike the Passive Aggressive types who readily involve themselves in the relative competition of dominance and submission (and sometimes sadomasochism), Resigned types remain relatively detached from such activities and only with difficulty can be stressed to an A+ state of active aggression. However, like Passive Aggressive types, the Resigned types can be induced into the aggressive-vindictive A rage.

The model denotes the state of resignation by –A, obtaining the following phenotypes:

- **Aggressive (–A)**
- **Perfectionistic-aggressive (P–A)**
- **Sanguine (N–A)**
- **Sanguine-perfectionistic (NP–A)**

The sanguine Resigned types, having the N trait, correspond to detached individuals, as described by Horney. She considered that "moving away from people" was a maladaptive response that could develop as a growing individual struggled toward maturity [14]. The *NP–A type* would tend to have strong perfectionistic tendencies, while the *N–A type* would be more labile.

Borderline types and mental illness

In the NPA model *Borderline types* possess only one of the traits of ambition (N or A) and it is only partially expressed. Types in which both traits (N and A) are either absent or profoundly suppressed fall into categories of mental illness, in particular schizophrenia [6]. Thus, NPA theory predicts that the categories of Borderline personality and schizophrenia are heterogeneous, depending on the underlying NPA character structure. Examples of Borderline types would be the A– or PA– types above. Types falling into the categories of mental illness would be the compliant submissive types, A= or PA=.

One aspect of the model focuses on the Dominant types N and NP, which lack the trait A [6]. In analogy with partial expression of the trait A, the theory identifies states of incomplete expression of the trait N, denoted as N–, N= and –N. Examples of Borderline types would be N– or N– P types. Types falling into the categories of mental illness would be N= or N=P, the latter being a perfectionistic, autistic individual.

Dominance and submission

In the NPA model, Dominant character types having the trait A have the potential of being reduced to an A– subdued state acutely or to a subjugated state chronically (see Fig. A1 above). Similarly, non-compliant Passive Aggressive types have the potential of being activated to an energetic A+ state resembling dominance, usually for short periods of time. Thus, the model emphasizes the potential lability of trait A in social relations, with Dominant and Passive Aggressive types continually altering their behavior in competitive interactions with other individuals and in the context of mating. In the extreme, some of these relationships fall into the category of sadomasochism [15]. Resigned types, in their detachment from social interactions, steadfastly avoid dominance-submission relationships and, in particular, hierarchal structures where "pecking orders" predominate.

Mendelian transmission of NPA traits

On the basis of archetypal examples, the model assumes that in their full expression the NPA traits are transmitted by autosomal genes, with traits A and N being recessive and trait P being transmitted in the dominant mode [6]. The alleles corresponding to full expression and total suppression of the trait A are denoted by **a** and A_0, respectively, and the corresponding alleles for the trait N are denoted by **n** and N_0. For the trait P two alleles **P** and p_0 are posited, corresponding to full expression or total absence of the trait P, on the assumption that the trait is transmitted with complete penetrance. This scheme of inheritance is consistent with the notion that the alleles A_0 and N_0 control the production of inhibitors of the traits A and N at the level of the central nervous system, with alleles A_0 and N_0 being dominant with respect to **a** and **n**. The scheme leads directly to Table A1, showing the possible phenotypes of progeny according to the phenotypes of the parents:

The table shows:

- N and A individuals need not have N or A parents. Such individuals can arise *de novo* so long as at least one of the parents is an NP and PA individual, respectively.
- PA individuals must have at least one parent who is of either the PA or A type.
- NP individuals must have at least one parent who is of either the NP or N type.
- NA individuals can arise *de novo* from any combination of phenotypes.
- The mating of two NA types can yield progeny of only NA types.

- The mating of an NPA type with an NA type can yield progeny of only NPA or NA types.

- Certain combinations of parental genotypes may lead to zygotes having only the P trait (P phenotype) or lacking all three traits (null phenotype, denoted by 0). According to NPA theory, zygotes of P or null phenotype would be non-viable. Thus, the model predicts partial or complete infertility in some combinations of parental phenotypes, these being N×A, N×PA, NP×A and NP×PA.

N	N -- -- NA -- -- -- -- --	"	"	"	"	"
A	N -- -- NA -- -- 0 A	-- -- -- NA -- -- -- A	"	"	"	"
NP	N NP -- NA NPA -- -- --	N NP P NA NPA PA 0 A	N NP -- NA NPA -- -- --	"	"	"
NA	N -- -- NA -- -- -- --	-- -- -- NA -- -- -- A	N NP -- NA NPA -- -- --	-- -- -- NA -- -- -- --	"	"
PA	N NP P NA NPA PA 0 A	-- -- -- NA NPA PA -- A	N NP P NA NPA PA 0 A	-- -- -- NA NPA PA -- A	-- -- -- NA NPA PA -- A	"
NPA	N NP -- NA NPA -- -- --	-- -- -- NA NPA PA -- A	N NP -- NA NPA -- -- --	-- -- -- NA NPA -- -- --	-- -- -- NA NPA PA -- A	-- -- -- NA NPA -- -- --
FATHER OR MOTHER	**N**	**A**	**NP**	**NA**	**PA**	**NPA**

Table A1. Possible phenotypes of children according to the phenotypes of the parents. The phenotypes of the father and mother are shown along the axes of the table. The P and null (0) phenotypes by the model are non-viable and would result in miscarriage, stillbirth or an infant who fails to thrive.

Implications of a trait theory based on genetics

Population Genetics

A trait theory based on genetics would imply that the personality structure of a population could be expressed in definitive mathematical terms. The NPA model is amenable to the Hardy-Weinberg approach to quantify the distribution of NPA character types in a given subpopulation [16]. With the usual assumptions of gene frequencies n, p and a and random mating, incidences of Dominant character types are given in Table A2, below. Because of the occurrence of non-viable P and null (0) phenotypes, the assumptions of Hardy-Weinberg equilibrium would not be strictly valid: the incidences generated by the expressions in Table A2 below represent the phenotypes of the first generation only.

The assumption of numerical values for the three gene frequencies n, p and a generates a hypothetical subpopulation, or habitancy [16]. In Table A3 six habitancies are given with descriptive labels: *Polymorphic,* (or "Balanced"), *Punctilious, Sublime, Demonstrative, Authoritarian* and *Militant*. The intent of the labels is to emphasize the very different tenors of each of the distributions of character types.

The table demonstrates that:

- Relatively small changes in gene frequencies could cause large changes in the phenotype frequencies.

- The frequencies of non-viable P and null types are low for these habitancies, on the order of 0 to 8 percent.

Relative incidence of phenotypes on basis of gene frequencies *n*, *p* and *a*

Phenotype	Relative incidence
N	$n^2 \times (1-p)^2 \times (1-a^2)$
A	$(1-n^2) \times (1-p)^2 \times a^2$
NP	$n^2 \times p(2-p) \times (1-a^2)$
NA	$n^2 \times (1-p)^2 \times a^2$
PA	$(1-n^2) \times p(2-p) \times a^2$
NPA	$n^2 \times p(2-p) \times a^2$
P	$2n(1-n) \times p(2-p) \times 2a(1-a)$
null (0)	$2n(1-n) \times (1-p)^2 \times 2a(1-a)$

Table A2. Relative incidences of phenotypes for the first generation. The incidence for each phenotype is the product of three probabilities, corresponding to the presence or absence of the three traits N, P and A. The P and null types are non-viable and contribute neither to parentage nor issue.

	HABITANCY					
Phenotype	Balanced	Punctilious	Sublime	Demonstrative	Authoritarian	Militant
N	7	3	77	2	1	1
A	3	<1	<1	2	17	34
NP	22	78	18	7	2	1
NA	13	<1	3	20	6	11
PA	9	2	<1	7	52	35
NPA	39	8	1	61	17	12
P	4	8	<1	1	4	2
null (0)	1	<1	1	<1	1	2
Gene frequencies	$n = 0.90$ $p = 0.50$ $a = 0.80$	$n = 0.90$ $p = 0.80$ $a = 0.30$	$n = 0.99$ $p = 0.10$ $a = 0.20$	$n = 0.95$ $p = 0.50$ $a = 0.95$	$n = 0.50$ $p = 0.50$ $a = 0.95$	$n = 0.50$ $p = 0.30$ $a = 0.95$

Table A3. Frequencies of phenotypes in six habitancies (per 100 zygotes, or pregnancies). The P and null (0) phenotypes are non-viable. Non-viable types arise when the zygote has neither trait N nor A. The above analysis is confined to Dominant character types on the assumption of two alleles for each NPA gene.

Evolutionary origins of NPA traits

The assumption of a genetic basis for the traits N, P and A implies that their origins reside in the evolution of humans from precursor species, and in particular, that the traits are likely to be found in primates other than *Homo sapiens*. As examples, the model leads to proposed character types as follows:

- The omnivorous, hierarchal, unsmiling olive baboon, known for its lengthy grooming rituals, would be a likely perfectionist-aggressive PA type.

- The herbivorous, aloof, phlegmatic orangutan and gorilla, capable of gingival smiles, would be likely NP types.

- Akin to humans, the omnivorous, promiscuous chimpanzee, also capable of the gingival smile, would likely have a heterogeneous distribution of types, with NA and NPA types predominating.

Fig. A4. NPA theory proposes that the olive baboon is a likely perfectionist-aggressive PA type.

Predictive aspects of NPA model

The model would have the potential to be predictive in the following categories:

- The possible genetic character types of children could be deduced from the character types of parents.

- Relations could be defined between genetic character type and susceptibility to certain physical and mental diseases.

- Combinations of parental character types prone to infertility problems (miscarriage and stillbirth) could be identified, these combinations being ones which permit the occurrence of a fetus having neither trait N nor A.

- Allele frequencies for the NPA traits, as well as the resultant distributions of NPA character types, in various societies could be analyzed on the basis of well-known principles of population genetics.

- Studies with primates could confirm a biological basis for behavior in the areas of sociobiology and evolutionary psychology.

Criticism and controversy

Controversy has always followed past positions taken by the scientific community relating human behavior to inheritance, as in Arthur Jensen's theories of intelligence, Herrnstein and Murray's "The Bell Curve", or Lewontin and colleagues' "Not in Our Genes". The NPA personality theory is not exempt. The result of the "nature versus nurture" debate has been that a gauntlet had been thrown to those who espouse genetic underpinnings to behavior: "show us the relevant genes".

The slow progress of unraveling of the genetic basis of personality is the subject of a recent review article by Jang and colleagues [2]. They point out the lack of any genetic framework in the classification of the Diagnostics and Statistical Manual of American psychiatry (DSM-IV), and the pressing need to identify "genetically crisp" characteristics — or genetic traits of behavior that are independent of competing genetic and environmental influences.

The NPA model posits narcissism to be a genetic trait, being related to the parasympathetic branch of the autonomic nervous system, just as aggression is classically related to the sympathetic branch. This concept of narcissism, and the associated narcissistic rage, is not found in any branch of classical medicine or psychiatry and remains a key point requiring validation. Of note is the recent study by Livesley and colleagues [3] with identical and fraternal twins. They found that of a total of eighteen dimensions of personality it was narcissism that had the highest heritability.

The manuscript of the NPA model was copyrighted with the Library of Congress in 1982, being published in book form in 1985 [17] and in a peer-reviewed journal in 1990 [6]. A revised electronic edition in pdf format was released in 2004 and the online NPA personality test in 2005. Studies are in progress utilizing the NPA personality test in obstetric and gynecological patients [18].

Although the NPA model is several decades old, it has not been validated in the sense of withstanding scrutiny by the scientific method — as is true of all other theories of personality as well. Given the recent advances in deciphering the human genome, such scrutiny may soon be possible. The ideas of Karen Horney have been resilient over time, and the validity of her observations that form the basis of the NPA model awaits the relevant studies in the realm of behavioral genetics.

References

Benis, A.M. *Toward Self and Sanity: On the genetic origins of the human character*, Psychological Dimensions, New York, 1985. ISBN 0884370747 [2nd edition, *The NPA Theory of Personality*, 2017. ISBN 9781521283295]

Benis, A.M. and J.H. Rand (1986). A model of human personality based on Mendelian genetics (abstract). *Proceedings of the American Association for the Advancement of Science,* Publication 86-5, 124.

Benis, A.M. (1990). A theory of personality traits leads to a genetic model for borderline types and schizophrenia. *Speculations in Science and Technology 13* (3), 167-175.

Freud, Sigmund. "Heredity and the aetiology of the neuroses," in *Early Psycho-analytic Publications,* Hogarth, London, [1896] 1962.

Horney, Karen. *Neurosis and Human Growth*, Norton, 1950.

Horney, Karen. *Our Inner Conflicts*, Norton, 1945.

Horney, Karen. *New Ways in Psychoanalysis*, Norton, 1939.

Horney, Karen. *Feminine Psychology*, Norton, [1922 to 1937] 1967.

Jang, K.L., Vernon, P.A. and W.J. Livesley (2001). Behavioural-genetic perspectives on personality function. *Canadian Journal of Psychiatry 46*, 234-244.

Livesley, W.J., Jang, K.L., Jackson, D.N. and P.A. Vernon (1993). Genetic and environmental contributions to dimensions of personality disorder. *American Journal of Psychiatry 150*, 1826-1831.

Stone, Michael H. *The Borderline Syndromes*, McGraw-Hill, 1980.

Citations

1. *Personality*, in Wikipedia.
2. Jang *et al.* (2001). Behavioural-genetic perspectives.
3. Livesley *et al.* (1993). Genetic and environmental contributions.
4. Horney, *Neurosis and Human Growth*, Chapter 8: The expansive solutions: the appeal of mastery.
5. Horney, *Neurosis and Human Growth*, Chapter 4: Neurotic pride.
6. Benis (1990). Theory of personality traits leads to genetic model.
7. Horney, *New Ways in Psychoanalysis*, Chapter 5: The concept of narcissism.

8. Horney, *Our Inner Conflicts*, Chapter 4: Moving against people.

9. Horney, *Feminine Psychology*, pp. 182-213.

10. Horney, *New Ways in Psychoanalysis*, p. 97.

11. Horney, *Our Inner Conflicts*, Chapter 12: Sadistic trends.

12. Horney, *New Ways in Psychoanalysis*, Chapter 15: Masochistic phenomena.

13. Horney, *Our Inner Conflicts*, Chapter 3: Moving toward people.

14. Horney, *Our Inner Conflicts*, Chapter 5: Moving away from people.

15. Horney, *Neurosis and Human Growth*, Chapter 10: Morbid dependency.

16. Benis, *Toward Self and Sanity*, Chapter 10: Genetics.

17. Benis, *Toward Self and Sanity*.

18. by Donna K. Hobgood, M.D., Clinical Attending Physician, University of Tennessee College of Medicine, Chattanooga.

Illustrations

Karen Horney: "Studio photo" courtesy of Karen Horney Papers, Manuscripts and Archives, Yale University Library, New Haven. Copyright unknown.

Character types according to theory of humors: From Johann Kaspar Lavater, *Physiognomics*, ca. 1775.

Olive baboon: U.S. Fish and Wildlife Service.

Source

This article originally appeared in *Wikipedia*, the online encyclopedia in May 2006. It was later deleted for reasons of non-notability. The reference was: "NPA personality theory", *Wikipedia, The Free Encyclopedia,* 2 July 2006, Wikimedia Foundation:

http://en.wikipedia.org/wiki/NPA_personality_theory.

APPENDIX B

Personal log of NPA types

Dominant

N	A
_____	_____
_____	_____
_____	_____
_____	_____
_____	_____
_____	_____
_____	_____
_____	_____
_____	_____
_____	_____
_____	_____
_____	_____
_____	_____
_____	_____
_____	_____
_____	_____
_____	_____
_____	_____
_____	_____
_____	_____
_____	_____

Dominant

NA

NP

Dominant

PA   NPA

Passive Aggressive
NPA−/= & NA−/=

_____

_____

_____

_____

_____

_____

_____

_____

_____

_____

_____

_____

_____

_____

_____

_____

_____

_____

_____

Resigned
NP−A & N−A

_____

_____

_____

_____

_____

_____

_____

_____

_____

_____

_____

_____

_____

_____

_____

_____

_____

_____

_____

GLOSSARY

aggression   The basis of human desire to survive by maintaining a position of power over competitors. Trait A of the model.

aggressive rage (A rage)   Mass discharge of the sympathetic nervous system related to the A trait of aggression.

allele   An alternative form of a gene at a given locus

autistic   Developmental disorders characterized by restricted and repetitive behavior that impair social interaction and communication.

autonomic nervous system   The portion of the nervous system governing many activities that are not under conscious control. It is composed of two parts: the *sympathetic* and *parasympathetic* nervous systems.

autosomal   Pertaining to a non-sex chromosome.

bipolar disorder   A major disorder of the emotional tone of the individual. It is characterized by severe mood swings toward mania, depression or both.

blushing   A response of flushing in an emotional context, in the skin of the face, neck and upper chest. According to the model, individuals having the N trait have an increased predisposition to blushing and flushing.

Borderline type   An NPA type in which neither trait N nor A is fully expressed.

breed true   A trait is said to breed true if two parents of the same phenotype always produce offspring of that same phenotype exclusively. The NA type is the only type of the model that always breeds true: any two NA types can have only NA offspring.

carrier   An individual who carries a gene that is not expressed. In the model, the non-aggressive N and NP types can be carriers of genes for the A− trait of inhibited aggression.

chromosomes   The cell structures containing the genetic material DNA. The human genome is composed of 46 chromosomes: 22 pairs of autosomes and 2 sex chromosomes.

cognition   The acts of thinking, feeling, knowing, reasoning and learning, including both awareness and judgment.

compliant type   A Passive Aggressive character type having profound inhibition of the A trait (denoted by A=).

dominant trait   Refers to Mendelian dominance. Not to be confused with *Dominant type*.

Dominant type   An NPA type in which the traits N and/or A are fully expressed. The six types are: N, A, NA, NP, PA and NPA.

energetic state   An individual having the A− trait can assume a transient energetic state resembling dominance (A+) by undergoing a *personality split*.

exhibitionism   Tendency toward display or extravagant behavior. Exhibitionism is most often a manifestation of the *unbridled* N trait.

explosive personality   A disorder characterized by volcanic outbursts of rage, or of verbal or physical aggressiveness.

expressivity   The degree to which a genetic trait is observed in the phenotype. Variable expressivity may be caused by modifier genes or by environmental effects.

extrovert   An individual whose attention and interests are directed primarily toward others.

failure to thrive   Refers to an infant who does not develop normally and eventually succumbs.

"fight-or-fight" reaction   Behavioral response associated with mass discharge of the *sympathetic nervous system*, as described by the American physiologist W.B. Cannon.

gene   A fundamental unit of heredity, composed mainly of DNA. Genes are arranged in linear order on the chromosomes.

genotype   The genetic constitution of alleles in an individual with respect to a gene locus or loci.

gingival smile   A broad smile, revealing the gums of the upper teeth, related to the N trait.

habitancy   In NPA population genetics, the inhabitants of a region, taken collectively, or a subpopulation. For ease of communication we define the following habitancies:

Polymorphic — a mixture of NPA character types
Sublime — mainly N types
Punctilious — ... NP types
Corybantic — ... NA types
Demonstrative — ... NPA types
Authoritarian — ... PA types
Militant — ... A types
Introspective — ... NPA– types

heterozygous   Having non-identical alleles at a locus of a homologous pair of chromosomes.

homozygous   Having identical alleles at a locus of a homologous pair of chromosomes.

Horney, Karen (1885–1952)   German-American psychiatrist of Dutch and Norwegian heritage.

hypomanic   In psychiatric terms, an individual who has a heightened emotional tone. In *mania* the individual is psychotic and usually requires hospitalization.

infertility   The relative inability of a mated couple to produce viable offspring.

introvert   An individual whose interests are predominantly concerned with his own mental life.

modifier genes   Genes that modify an observed physical or behavioral trait.

morbid dependency   A symbiotic relationship based on the trait of aggression, essentially sadomasochistic in nature, between individuals assuming dominant and submissive roles.

narcissism   From Narcissus, the figure in Greek mythology who fell in love with his own reflected image. In the present model, narcissism is related to the N trait of sanguinity.

narcissistic arms gesture   A gesture of recognition in which the arms are extended to the front or sides, with the fingers slightly spread apart.

narcissistic personality disorder (NPD)   In the NPA model patients diagnosed with NPD will likely be individuals having the *unbridled* N trait..

narcissistic rage (N rage)   Mass discharge of the autonomic nervous system related to the N trait of sanguinity.

non-compliant type   A Passive Aggressive character type having partial inhibition of the A trait (denoted by A−).

non-sanguine   Refers to individuals who lack the trait N.

paranoia   A behavioral pattern characterized by hyper-sensitivity, suspicion, jealousy, envy and a tendency to blame others and ascribe evil motives to them.

parsimony, principle of   The explanation most likely to be correct is the one that explains the greatest number of observations with the fewest number of assumptions. Also referred to as "Occam's razor".

"passive-aggressive"   A behavioral pattern characterized by obstructionism, procrastination and intentional inefficiency. Not to be confused with *Passive Aggressive type.*

Passive Aggressive type   An NPA type in which trait A is genetically partially inhibited.

penetrance   The expression of a trait when the genotype is present. Thus, in "incomplete penetrance" a certain proportion of individuals will not exhibit the trait although the appropriate genotype is present.

perfectionism   The P trait of the model, appearing in behavior as 1) the achievement of order by persistence and repetition, and 2) as a trait that modulates the expression of the unbridled N and A traits.

personality   A collection of behavioral patterns unique to an individual that is consistent over time.

personality split   According to the model, individuals having the A or A− trait may transiently assume the converse subdued (A−) and energetic (A+) states, respectively.

phenocopy   A phenotype in which environmental factors result in a trait similar to one caused by a genetic mechanism. In the model, the A– trait may be caused by an **a-** gene, but there may also occur phenocopies of this trait based on adverse factors during an individual's period of nurture.

phenotype   The observable traits in an individual. The NPA character types (N, NP, NA–, etc.) are phenotypes.

"playing the game"   Individuals having a measure of the trait of aggression constantly "play the game" of dominance and submission.

pleiotropism   The determination of multiple characteristics by a single gene.

polygenic   Referring to the influence of several genes determining the expression of a trait.

power behind throne   A symbiotic relationship between a PA individual (the Power) and a figurehead individual on whom he depends.

psychosis   A major mental disorder in which the individual's ability to interpret reality is grossly impaired.

recessive trait   Refers to a trait that is expressed only when the causative gene is present in the homozygous state, i.e., on both chromosomes of an autosomal pair. See *dominant trait*.

resignation   The state denoted –A in which an individual at maturity renounces the "playing of the game" of dominance and submission and adopts a philosophy of serene independence.

Resigned type   An NPA type in which trait A is inhibited by environmental factors after maturity in an individual who was formerly either 1) a Dominant A, PA, NA or NPA type, or 2) a Passive Aggressive type.

sadism   Satisfaction derived from aggressively dominating or abusing others.

sadomasochism   A symbiotic relationship between two individuals based on the trait of aggression.

sanguine, sanguinity According to ancient physiology, belonging to one of the "four temperaments" in which blood predominates over the other three "humors", leading to a ruddy countenance and exuberant behavior. In the NPA model a sanguine personality type is any type having the N trait.

schizoid Withdrawn; tending to avoid close relationships with others.

smile According to the model, the social smile of recognition is based on the N trait of sanguinity.

subdued state An individual having fully expressed trait A can be reduced to a transient subdued state resembling submission (A–) by undergoing a *personality split*.

subjugated state A chronic state resembling submission (A–) of an individual with respect to a stronger companion or mate.

Submissive type A compliant Passive Aggressive character type who adopts a life style of deference to others.

symbiosis A relationship between two individuals that has elements of mutual advantage.

sympathetic nervous system A division of the autonomic nervous system that controls the "fight-or-flight" response related to the trait of aggression.

synergy An enhanced effect on behavior, for example when the unbridled N and A traits complement each other in the NA type.

temperament The general level of activity, reactivity or excitability of an individual in the Pavlovian sense.

unbridled trait The presence of fully expressed trait N or A without modulation by the P trait.

REFERENCES & NOTES

Chapter 1: Personality Is Inherited

[*1*] See Appendix A: *NPA Personality Theory: Synopsis*. This article, originally published in Wikipedia, is a concise summary of the NPA model.

Chapter 2: The Three Traits: N, P and A

[*2*] Horney (1945, 1950); Benis (1990); See also Appendix A.

[*3*] Benis (1985/2017). (This is the original published version of the NPA theory.) See also Appendix A.

[*4*] Benis (1990). See also Appendix A: *Synopsis: Borderline types.*

Borderline types in the NPA model are those in which neither trait N nor trait A is fully expressed. This would include the non-sanguine Passive Aggressive types A− and PA−, as well as the non-aggressive N− and N−P types in which the N trait is not fully expressed. Borderline types are considered to be "borderline" in the sense that are very close genetically to the non-viable P and null types, in which the N and A traits are completely absent. In general, Borderline types are considered to be behaviorally impaired in contemporary Western society, where social relations are often based on competition. In this book, we do not consider the possibility of Borderline as parents. However, the do arise naturally as progeny in some matings, as for example in matches of a non-sanguine Dominant type with a sanguine Passive Aggressive type (like PA×NPA−), for which the progeny would include the Borderline Passive Aggressive types A− and PA−.

[*5*] Published originally in Benis (1985/2017). See also Benis (2017b): *Caricatures of the NPA Personality Types.*

[*6*] Benis (2017a): *Geographic Distribution of Genetic Character Traits Based on the NPA Theory of Personality.* See also Appendix A.

Chapter 3: Dominant Types

[*7*] Published originally in Benis (1985/2017). See also Benis (2017b): *Caricatures of the NPA Personality Types.*

Chapter 4: Inhibited Aggression: Passive Aggressive Types

[*8*] We do not include here the non-sanguine Passive Aggressive types A−, PA−, A= and PA=. The non-compliant A− and PA− types are Borderline types, while the compliant A= and PA= types would be classified as mentally ill. For details see Benis (1990): "A theory of

personality traits leads to a genetic model for borderline types and schizophrenia." See also Appendix A.

[*9*] Published originally in Benis (1985/2017). See also Benis (2017b): *Caricatures of the NPA Personality Types.*

Chapter 5: Inhibited Aggression: Resigned Types

[*10*] We do not include here the non-sanguine Resigned types −A and P−A. Since these types have neither trait N nor A fully expressed, they would be classified as Borderline types or mentally ill. For details see Benis (1990): "A theory of personality traits leads to a genetic model for borderline types and schizophrenia." See also Appendix A.

[*11*] Published originally in Benis (1985/2017). See also Benis (2017b): *Caricatures of the NPA Personality Types.*

[12] Excerpts from the works of Maugham (1930, 1932) related to Resigned types are included in Benis (1985/2017). A remarkable essay by Maugham on Resigned types is buried in *The Gentleman in the Parlour*, an account of his travels in the Far East.

Chapter 6: Inheritance of the NPA Traits

[*13*] Benis (1985/2017). The unusual mechanism of transmission for N and A, as high-frequency *recessive* traits, leads to the hypothesis that these loci code for inhibitors of the traits, and that an inactive inhibitor would lead to a "release of inhibition" allowing expression of that trait. Thus, the genetic loci for traits N and A likely code for inhibitors of the traits. For trait A, the model implies that whatever the complexity of the many possible genes that permit the expression and modulation of the trait of aggression, it is a single genetic locus (the A locus of the NPA model) that permits inhibition of the final common pathway to expression of the A trait and A rage, permitting the occurrence of the non-aggressive N and NP types of the model. For trait N, the model implies that whatever the complexity of the genes that permit the expression and modulation of the trait of sanguinity, it is a single genetic locus (the N locus of the NPA model) that permits inhibition of the final common pathway to expression of the N trait and N rage, permitting the occurrence of the non-sanguine A and PA types.

Note that in this book we use the recessive alleles **n** and **a,** rather than their matched dominant alleles **No** and **Ao** that are assumed to code for the absence of traits N and A, respectively.

[*14*] In the category of *partial infertility,* one such parental combination would be a match of the genotypes **(nP/nP)×(nPa/Pa),** which would

correspond to a mating NP×PA. About fifty percent of the issue would be of genotype **(nP/Pa),** hence non-viable. In the category of *complete infertility,* an example would be the match **(n/nP)×(a/Pa),** which would again correspond to a mating NP×PA. Such a union could give issue only to progeny of genotype **(na),** i.e., null type, or **(nPa)** and **(nPPa),** i.e., P types.

[*15*] Given the recessive transmission of fully expressed trait A and the likelihood that the A_0 locus codes for an inhibitor of the trait, we posited that a possible **a-** allele at the A locus itself could code for partial inhibition of the A trait, hence for the A− trait (Benis, 1990). However, given the complexity of the adrenergic neurotransmitters that are likely involved in the expression of trait A, the model allows for the alternative possibility that there may be multiple distinct genetic "A− loci" that modulate trait A by mechanisms of epistasis. In either case, we posit that the A− trait would not be expressed in the absence of trait A. However, although the non-aggressive N and NP types would be "silent" carriers of the A− trait with respect to the trait of aggression, this would not preclude the possibility of the **a-** allele's showing pleiotropism, and nevertheless being phenotypically expressed in some other manner unrelated to aggression.

Chapter 9: Conclusion

[*16*] Our web site address is npatheory.com. One can post on the Message Board, or submit material via the "contact" link.

BIBLIOGRAPHY

Benis, A.M. (1985). *Toward Self & Sanity: On the genetic origins of the human character,* Psychological Dimensions, New York. Revised edition (2017), as *NPA Theory of Personality*, New York, ISBN 978-1521283295.

Benis A.M. (2017a). *Geographic Distribution of Genetic Character Traits Based on the NPA Theory of Personality*, KDP/Amazon, ISBN 978-1520430317.

Benis A.M. (2017b). *Caricatures of the NPA Personality Types*, KDP/Amazon, ISBN 978-1520966977.

Benis A.M. (2017c). *NPA Personality Theory: The Essentials*, KDP/Amazon, ISBN 978-1521399910.

Benis A.M. (1990). A theory of personality traits leads to a genetic model for borderline types and schizophrenia. *Speculations in Science and Technology* 13 (3), 167-75.

Horney K. (1950). *Neurosis and Human Growth*, Norton, New York.

Horney, K. (1945). *Our Inner Conflicts*, Norton, New York.

Maugham W.S. (1932). *The Narrow Corner,* Doubleday, New York.

Maugham W.S. (1930). *The Gentleman in the Parlour,* Doubleday, New York.

ACKNOWLEDGEMENTS

The author thanks D.K. Hobgood, M.D. for her helpful comments and sustained interest. J.H. Rand, M.D. provided invaluable assistance with the original version of the NPA model and helped to guide the manuscript to the publisher.

SOURCES OF ILLUSTRATIONS

Figure 1, p. 12:

Barack Obama by DonkeyHotey. Creative Commons license via Wikipedia Commons File: 2012 Obama Romney caricature.jpg.

Vladimir Putin by DonkeyHotey. Creative Commons license via: Wikipedia Commons File: Vladimir Putin - Olympic Host.jpg.

Angela Merkel by DonkeyHotey. Creative Commons license via: flickr.com/photos/donkeyhotey/12952652895.

Richard Cheney by DonkeyHotey. Creative Commos license via: flickr.com/photos/donkeyhotey/16011605976.

Christopher Christie by DonkeyHotey. Creative Commons license via: flickr.com/photos/donkeyhotey/9529109477.

Adele Adkins. Digital painting by Carsten S., Berlin, Germany. Creative Commons license via: flickr.com/photos/caschie/25600151946.

Figure 2, p. 56:

Charles Darwin, ca. 1854. Filtered image from source photograph in public domain, via Wikipedia Commons File: Charles Darwin seated crop.jpg.

Elizabeth Warren by DonkeyHotey. Creative Commons license via: flickr.com/photos/donkeyhotey/13906218886.

Figure 3, p. 69:

Michael Jackson. Wikipedia images via: fr.wikipedia.org/wiki/Filmographie_de_Michael_Jackson.

Cover

Image from kambodza. Creative Commons license via: flickr.com/photos/49507393@N08/4535874193/

INDEX

ABOUT THE AUTHOR

The author received the degree of Doctor of Science from MIT. His medical training was at the Mount Sinai Medical Center in New York, where he served afterward for many years as Research Associate Professor and Director of Cardiothoracic Intensive Care. He is the author of a number of research papers and review articles. His interest in the genetics of personality grew with his experience with families in the intensive care environment.